DEFYING CONVENTION
WOMEN WHO CHANGED THE RULES

WOMEN
IN TECHNOLOGY

ELIZABETH SCHMERMUND

Enslow Publishing
101 W. 23rd Street
Suite 240
New York, NY 10011
USA

enslow.com

Published in 2017 by Enslow Publishing, LLC.
101 W. 23rd Street, Suite 240, New York, NY 10011

Library of Congress Cataloging-in-Publication Data

Names: Schmermund, Elizabeth, author.
Title: Women in technology / Elizabeth Schmermund.
Description: New York, NY, USA : Enslow Publishing, 2017. | Series: Defying convention : women who changed the rules | Includes bibliographical references and index.
Identifiers: LCCN 2016021790 | ISBN 9780766081499 (library bound)
Subjects: LCSH: Women in technology—History—Juvenile literature. | Technology—History—Juvenile literature.
Classification: LCC T36 .S36 2017 | DDC 609.2/52—dc23
LC record available at https://lccn.loc.gov/2016021790

Printed in Malaysia

To Our Readers: We have done our best to make sure all websites in this book were active and appropriate when we went to press. However, the author and the publisher have no control over and assume no liability for the material available on those websites or on any websites they may link to. Any comments or suggestions can be sent by e-mail to customerservice@enslow.com.

Photo Credits: Cover (top left), p. 20 Universal Images Group/Getty Images; cover (top right), p. 111 Jerod Harris/WireImage/Getty Images; cover (bottom left) Bloomberg/Getty Images; cover (bottom right) pp. 5, 83 Bettmann/Getty Images; p. 13 Science Source; p. 17, 30 Hulton Archive/Getty Images; pp. 24-25 Insung Jeon/Moment/Getty Images; p. 35 Leemage/Universal Images Group/Getty Images; p. 39 PHAS/Universal Images Group/Getty Images; p. 41 Archive Photos/Getty Images; p. 48 De Agostini/S. Vannini/Getty Images; pp. 51, 63 De Agostini/A. Dagli Orti/Getty Images; p. 54 Science Museum/SSPL/Getty Images; pp. 57, 65 Science & Society Picture Library/Getty Images; p. 60 SPL/Science Source; p. 69 Science Source/Getty Images; p. 72 Harold M. Lambert/Archive Photos/Getty Images; p. 74 Harvard College Observatory/Science Source; p. 78 Topical Press Agency/Hulton Archive/Getty Images; p. 81 Ralph Morse/The LIFE Picture Collection/Getty Images; p. 88 Robert Coburn/Moviepix/Getty Images; p. 92 Photo Researchers/Science Source/Getty Images; p. 98 NurPhoto/Getty Images; p. 101 Archive Photos/Getty Images; p. 105 Scientist-100/Wikimedia Commons/File:Radia Perlman 2009.jpg/Public Domain; p. 108 © AP Images

CONTENTS

Historically, women inventors and innovators have often not received the attention they have deserved, although they have been driving forces in the technological advances that continue to revolutionize our world. In fact, women have invented many of the important technologies that we use in the twenty-first century. Women like Grace Hopper developed computer programming when computers were in their infancy. Women like Katherine Johnson created important technologies in the race to put the first man (and woman) in space.

In fact, one of the first computer programmers and the founder of scientific computing is Augusta Ada King, countess of Lovelace, known more popularly as Ada Lovelace. Lovelace passed away in 1852 without ever seeing the exciting developments her work would inspire—or receiving proper recognition for her foundational contribution to what we now call computer science.

Nearly one hundred years later, in 1946, six women programmed the first electronic computer during World War II. Called the ENIAC, this computer (funded by the US Army) was built to calculate missile trajectories during the war. The trajectories had previously been manually calculated by a group of eighty female mathematicians!

Women were instrumental in war operations during World War II, programming the ENIAC to calculate missile trajectories.

These six women worked long days, attempting to program the first electronic computer in history. At the end of their project, ENIAC was able to calculate perfect ballistics trajectories. Kay Mauchley Antoinelli, Jean Bartik, Betty Holberton, Marlyn Meltzer, Frances Spence, and Ruth Teitelbaum remained largely unknown for their contributions to computer science until 1997, when they were inducted into the Hall of Fame of Women in Technology International (WITI). In tribute to the women, Anna van Raaphorst-Johnson, WITI's director, stated: "Somebody else stood up and took credit at the time, and no one looked back. It's a typical problem in a male-dominated industry. And there's still a lot of frustration with men taking credit for women's ideas—it doesn't seem to have changed much over the last fifty years."[1]

Too often, women's accomplishments in a male-dominated industry such as technology go unacknowledged. While this still occurs today, the path-breaking careers of innovative women and, in particular, their strength, dedication, talent, and persistence in the face of many challenges have opened up many more opportunities for women in tech. Today, women are the presidents, founders, and CEOs of large tech companies that are actively innovating technology that will change our world. This would not have been possible but for the previous work of many women who were never properly recognized.

This resource profiles many women whose contributions are ignored or forgotten, showing that women have been inventing since the beginning of recordable history and will continue to do so in the face of all of the odds.

CHAPTER ONE

WOMEN AND TECHNOLOGY IN THE ANCIENT WORLD

We don't equate "technology" with the ancient world, but ancient inventions helped revolutionize the way ancient peoples lived their lives—and paved the way for the newer technologies that we make use of today.

Across the ancient world—from Greece, to Egypt, to Mesopotamia, to China and beyond— women contributed to science, medicine, and technology. However, today most of their names are lost to time. In the Old Kingdom of ancient Egypt (ca. 2778–2263 BCE) women owned property, worked as scribes, and practiced medicine. In fact, medicine and medical technology in particular were the domain of women. Because women in many of these ancient cultures often aided one another in childbirth, rearing children, and taking care of the sick and the elderly, women were the first bastions of medical knowledge. In the ancient city of Heliopolis, in Egypt, for example, there was a women-only medical school that was known far and wide for the women's expertise and their ability to train students. In fact, an inscription on a temple at Memphis reads: "I have come from the school of medicine at Heliopolis, and have studied at the woman's school at Sais where the divine mothers have taught me how to cure disease."[1]

Written documents, called papyri, from this period reveal the extent of medical and technological knowledge these "divine mothers" possessed; they knew how to diagnose pregnancy and test for sterility or other gynecological problems, performed cesarean sections and mastectomies, and could even use splints to set broken bones.

In the great Sumerian civilization, women also enjoyed relative autonomy. In ancient Babylon around 2000 BCE, women could become judges and owned their own businesses. They, also, were pioneers in the fields of medicine and medical technology. However, Sumerian women were known in particular for their technological advancements in one field: perfume making. Ancient Sumerian women developed complex chemical techniques to make perfume, which are today known as distillation, extraction, and sublimation. Unfortunately, we don't know much about these intriguing women. Two of these early chemists, however, are named on ancient tablets: Tapputi-Belatekallim and Ninu.

In ancient Greece, however, women had less power and autonomy. Greece was made up of different city-states, the largest being Athens and Sparta. In Sparta, whose power was based upon its military strength, women were trained as warriors and had some degree of freedom. Not so in Athens, however. In Athens, the birthplace of democracy and Western philosophy, most women were not allowed out in public alone and were not allowed to own property, to operate businesses, or to work (except as prostitutes). In fact, a famous philosopher of the city, Aristotle, would argue that women were only "deformed" men—and had little merit of their own. This misogyny would become solidified across Western civilization. Throughout a period of rapid medical advancements in ancient Greece, attributed to the "father" of modern medicine, Hippocrates (ca. 460–370 BCE), women were not allowed within medical schools.

According to ancient records, around 300 BCE a Greek woman named Agnodice disguised herself as a man and traveled to Alexandria, Egypt, in order to learn medicine. Back in Athens, she set up a successful medical practice where she used current medical technology—such as surgery, splinting, and medicines—to heal her patients. Competing physicians who were jealous of her success started rumors that she stole away men's wives from them. In order to refute this baseless rumor, Agnodice revealed that she was a woman. She would have been condemned to death if not for the appeals of "noble women, [who] ... entered before the judges, and told them they would no longer account them for husbands and friends, but for cruel enemies that condemned her to death who restored to them their health, protesting they would all die with her if she were put to death."[2]

The women's tactic worked, Agnodice was spared from death, and, from then on, free, noble women were allowed to practice medicine in Athens—if, and only if, their only patients were women.

Women's status did not improve much during the rise of the Roman Empire, either. Following the decline of the Greek Empire, the Roman Empire rose to prominence in the early first century. Women were little more than slaves to the Romans, although upper-class women were often highly educated in ancient languages and philosophy. After the Romans conquered Greece, Greek female doctors were brought back to Rome and their knowledge was incorporated into the empire's. Soon, medical schools began to develop and women were allowed to become physicians. In fact, gradually, female physicians were allowed to practice on not only women, but men and children, too. In particular, these Roman female doctors advanced the field of gynecology.

While medical technologies were often developed and implemented by women, these ancient women also contributed to another important field: alchemy. Alchemy was the science that developed before chemistry in the ancient world and gained even more importance during the Middle Ages (ca. 400 to 1400). These alchemists worked secretly in attempts to turn common metals into silver and gold, at least to create alloys to make common metals look like more precious metals. But, while this process sounds more like magic than anything else, they really investigated physical processes and invented chemical compounds. Many scholars believe that this interest in alchemy, which flourished in Alexandria during the Egyptian Empire, actually began in ancient Babylon with women in the perfume industry. In fact, early alchemy was often called *opus mulierum*, which means "women's work" in Latin.

MARIA THE JEWESS

Today, scholars know a little bit about the woman who created the basis for Western alchemy and, thus, for the modern science of chemistry, which it would transform into. Maria the Jewess, who wrote her treatises as Miriam the Prophetess, is believed to have lived in Alexandria, Egypt, during the beginning of the first century.

Not only did Maria the Jewess write many influential publications about alchemy, some of which survive today, but she invented the necessary equipment that alchemists would continue to use for hundreds—if not thousands—of years.

While it is difficult for scholars to determine with complete accuracy if Maria the Jewess was the first inventor of these early pieces of equipment, they are attributed to her by several of her contemporary writers. In particular, Maria the Jewess invented three influential devices: the *tribikos*, the *kerotakis*, and what we refer to today as the bain-marie.

The tribikos is an earthenware container with three arms. The main container holds liquid to be distilled, while three metal spouts transfer the distilled liquid into glass vials. When the liquid inside the tribikos was heated, it would be turned into a gas that would rise out of the main container. As it touched the arms above the main container, the liquid would condense and fall into the glass vials. This device is still used today in chemistry labs to separate substances in liquids. In her writings, Maria the Jewess advised that the arms should be made of copper or bronze and that the sections, or joints, between the main container and the metal spouts should be sealed with a paste made from flour. Her instructions were incredibly detailed, and her knowledge was gained by years of experimentation.

The woman known as Maria the Jewess was an influential alchemist and is believed to have invented important equipment that is used in the field of chemistry.

The kerotakis was originally used as a "triangular palette" by artists to mix paints, which Maria the Jewess used to soften metals and then color them.[3] She reformed the device to include a cylindrical container that could be held over a fire, along with the original palette to hold the softened metals. According to author Margaret Alic:

Sulphur, mercury or arsenic sulphide solutions were heated in a pan near the bottom [of the cylinder]. Near the top of the cylinder, suspended from the cover, was the palette containing a copper-lead alloy (or other metal) to be treated. As the sulphur or mercury boiled, the vapour condensed at the top of the cylinder and the liquid flowed back down, thus establishing a continuous reflux. The sulphur vapours of the condensate attacked the metal alloy yielding a black sulphide—"Mary's Black"—thought to represent the first state of transmutation ... Continued heating eventually yielded a gold-like alloy.[4]

The bain-marie, which in French means "Mary's bath" and which is named after Maria the Jewess, is still an essential piece of laboratory and kitchen equipment today, nearly two thousand years after its invention. Essentially a double boiler, this device is used to heat a substance slowly and to keep its heat constant by heating it over water. In fact, some people still refer to the double boiler as a bain-marie today, and it is used for delicate kitchen operations such as melting chocolate.

Most of Maria the Jewess's work was lost in the third century, when the texts of alchemists were targeted for burning by the Roman emperor Diocletian. Because of this—and the continuing persecution of alchemists—advances in laboratory equipment were not made until the seventeenth century. Maria the Jewess's contributions to the field of alchemy and to laboratory equipment later used in chemistry would remain unchanged for nearly two thousand years.

CLEOPATRA THE ALCHEMIST (CA. 3RD CENTURY)

Cleopatra the Alchemist was an Egyptian alchemist and philosopher who lived during the third century. Cleopatra the Alchemist seems to have been influenced by Maria the Jewess, and she also contributed greatly to the burgeoning field of alchemy, the ancient precursor to chemistry. Cleopatra is the pseudonym for this powerful female scientist and inventor, whose real name is not known—however, she is not the same figure as the pharaoh Cleopatra.

Cleopatra the Alchemist invented the alembic, which is two containers connected by a tube used for distilling chemicals. As the liquid in one vessel heats up, it rises through the metal tube where it hits the sides of the metal, begins to cool, and then falls into the other vessel. Today, the alembic is still used to make cognac, an alcoholic drink that is made from distilling white wine.

The only remaining work of Cleopatra's that has survived nearly two thousand years, including the burning of many of these Egyptian texts following the Egyptian persecution of alchemists, is the *Chrysopoeia of Cleopatra*. This literally means "Cleopatra's gold-making," and it uses many illustrations to explain both Cleopatra's philosophical ideas and her alchemy experiments to turn base metals into gold and silver. In this text, Cleopatra included illustrations that show the technical processes of furnaces (some say that she was known for producing heat "magically" with horse manure), along with more abstract or spiritual illustrations. Scholars note that the *Chrysopoeia of Cleopatra* includes the earliest drawing of the ouroboros, which shows a snake eating its own tail. The ouroboros became a widely used symbol in alchemical texts and supposedly symbolized the circular nature of the alchemist's work—transforming plain rocks into precious metals and back again. The ouroboros has become an important symbol in mystical traditions such as Gnosticism.

Other ancient texts reveal that Cleopatra, along with Maria the Jewess and two other women, Taphnutia and Medera, were the only women who knew how to produce the philosopher's stone—which supposedly was not only the secret ingredient to turn base metals into gold and silver, but also granted its owners immortality and eternal youth. While Cleopatra the Alchemist is one of the few ancient women for whom we have a complete copy of her most important work, little else is

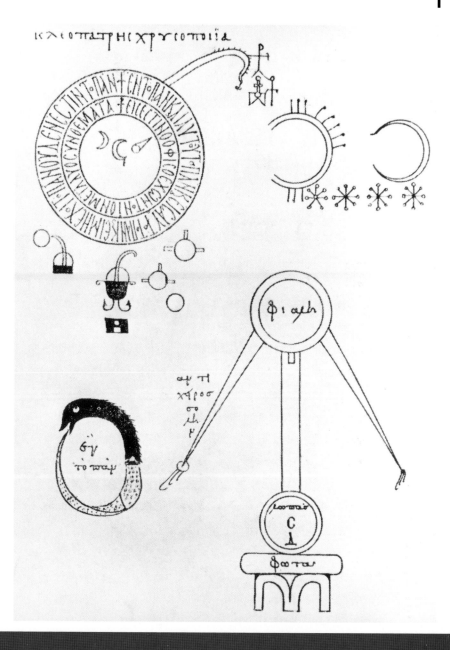

These symbols of alchemy are taken from the manuscript *Chrysopoeia of Cleopatra*. The ourobouros appears at the lower left.

known about her personal life, including the exact dates of her birth and death.

HYPATIA OF ALEXANDRIA (CA. 350–4150)

A lot more is known about a woman named Hypatia of Alexandria. Daughter of the famous mathematician Theon Alexandricus and born in Athens, Hypatia became one of the most important mathematicians, astronomers, and philosophers in world history. Hypatia is as well known for her important contributions to science, math, and ancient technology as for her brutal death: she was murdered by a mob in Alexandria because of increasing political and religious tensions between Cyril, the bishop of Alexandria, and Orestes, the governor of Alexandria, as well as between Christians and Jews. An angry mob that believed Hypatia was a symbol of Roman rule stoned her to death in 415 CE.

But while Hypatia was brutally killed by her contemporaries, her contributions have withstood the test of time. Hypatia was born and educated in Athens in the middle of the fourth century. Around 400 CE, she was appointed head of a school in Alexandria, Egypt, and moved there to teach. She taught about the important Greek philosophers, particularly Plato and Aristotle, as well as mathematical theorems.

In addition to her teaching and writings, Hypatia is credited with the invention of the hydrometer, a device used to measure the relative density of liquids, which is expressed in the ratio of a specific liquid's density to the density of water. In a letter between Hypatia and the Greek bishop Synesius of Cyrene, the hydrometer is described:

> The instrument in question is a cylindrical tube, which has the shape of a flute and is about the same size. It has notches in a perpendicular line, by means of which we are able to test the weight of the waters. A cone forms a lid at one of the extremities, closely fitted to the tube. The cone and the tube have one in the base only. This is called the beryllium. Whenever you place the tube in water, it remains erect. You can then count the notches at your ease; in this way ascertain the weight of the water.[5]

However, the most important invention normally attributed to Hypatia is the astrolabe. The astrolabe was a revolutionary technology in the ancient world. In fact, it actually functioned as an early computer, designed to calculate and predict the position of the sun and stars in the

Hypatia of Alexandria is acknowledged as the inventor of the astrolabe, a device that could predict the position of heavenly bodies. Hypatia is also renowned as a philosopher.

night sky. Typically, the astrolabe, often a round watchlike device made of bronze, featured a visual representation of celestial objects on its face. The owner could change the position of these objects on the astrolabe, which would then reposition the other celestial objects in the "sky." Using this, one could tell time, calculate the time of the sunrise or sunset, and map the stars in the sky—thus, eventually, determining one's latitude.

Unfortunately, none of Hypatia's original texts exist today, which makes it difficult for scholars to know for sure what she invented. However, some letters written by Synesius to Hypatia and to other ancient thinkers still exist. One letter, written by Synesius to a friend, states: "I am therefore offering you a gift most befitting for me to give, and for you to receive. It is a work of my own devising, including all that she [Hypatia], my most revered teacher, helped to contribute, and it was executed by the best hand to be found in our country in the art of the silversmith."[6]

In fact, other letters show that Theon, Hypatia's father and a famous inventor and mathematician in his own right, had already written a treatise on the astrolabe. Today, scholars state that while Hypatia may not have invented the first astrolabe, she most likely significantly contributed to its more elaborate functioning and design.

Hypatia's fame has never dwindled, and her contributions to mathematics, philosophy, and technology continue to inspire generations of women. Feminist philosophers have reclaimed Hypatia as a feminist inspiration, dedicating an important academic journal, *Hypatia: A Journal of Feminist Philosophy,* to her memory. In 1976, artist Judy Chicago created an art installation called *The Dinner Party*, made up of thirty-nine place settings around a triangular table that symbolize the important contributions of women in history. Hypatia's place setting is number thirteen, following such important ancient figures as Ishtar and Sappho. The installation is on permanent exhibition at the Elizabeth A. Sackler Center for Feminist Art at the Brooklyn Museum in Brooklyn, New York.

SONDOK (CA. 7TH CENTURY)

In the seventh century, a woman named Sondok became queen of the Kingdom of Silla in modern-day South Korea. Because her father had not had any sons, he granted his kingdom to his oldest daughter upon his death. During this time in Korea, women had relative amounts of power:

they acted as advisers to rulers and even ruled over land themselves. Within families, power, prestige, and inheritance often passed down through the mother's bloodline. Confucianism would not emerge as a religion for nearly one thousand years, which is when women's statuses would change more drastically and they began to take on more subordinate roles.

Sondok ruled Korea for fourteen years; during this time she expanded the influence of her kingdom. More important from a technological standpoint, Sondok was incredibly interested in both astronomy and Buddhism. She funded the building of many temples and observatories across her land. One of the most impressive buildings commissioned by Sondok is the "Tower of the Moon and Stars," which is considered the first astronomical observatory in the Far East. Named the Cheomseongdae, which means "the star-gazing tower" in Korean, this tower was constructed from 362 pieces of granite and stands 9.4 meters (30.8 feet) tall. The tower still stands today in Gyeongju, which was near the ancient capital of Silla. It is testament to the powerful rule of Sondok and to her quest for astronomical—and perhaps spiritual—discovery.

Back in the seventh century, many cultures viewed the stars and planets in the night sky as

The Cheomseongdae, known as the "Tower of the Moon and Stars," was commissioned by Sondok in the seventh century. The observatory still stands today in Gyeongju, South Korea.

being magical or signs sent by the gods. Queen Sondok was no different. While the astronomical observatory that she had built would help early astronomers to map out the sky, Sondok most likely thought that it would help her convene with a higher power. Indeed, Sondok was viewed not only as a powerful ruler in the Kingdom of Silla, but also as a shaman with powers to bring human beings and gods in contact. Sondok's power as a great ruler largely came from this claim to the gods, and Sondok was revered during her time for being able to anticipate events before they occurred.

CHAPTER TWO

WOMEN'S INNOVATIONS DURING THE MIDDLE AGES

I n Europe during the Middle Ages, which lasted approximately from the fifth century to the fifteenth century, women's roles differed greatly depending on their social status. During this time, most people lived in rural communities across Europe. For this reason, many peasant women shared in roles equal to that of men: farming, taking care of domestic responsibilities, cooking, and brewing beer (which was largely the role of women), in addition to child rearing and caretaking.

While there was certainly a gendered division of labor, which means that men and women took on different roles, women would occasionally take on jobs performed by their husbands during the busy seasons, such as working in the fields during the harvest. Women who lived in towns, instead of the countryside, also had some level of autonomy over their lives. They produced many goods, such as leather, textiles, and metalwork, and helped to run businesses such as shops and inns. While women did not have the same power over their lives as men did, they actively and importantly contributed to their villages, towns, and the larger economy.

Many women during the early Middle Ages (ca. 400–900 CE) inherited land or managed their properties while their husbands were away at war or on pilgrimages. Depending on where they were born—Europe, of course, is a vast expanse of territory that covers many cultural and geographical boundaries—a family's inheritance would either be passed down to the eldest child, regardless of sex, or to the eldest son.

While peasant women did have some level of autonomy, their lives were incredibly difficult. Also, women in the higher social classes actually had less power over their own lives. They were often married at a young age and were restricted to the home. This is not to say that there weren't women who held powerful and public positions. During this time, women took on powerful roles as queens and regents and ruled vast swaths of land while their husbands were away or when their sons were too young to take the crown.

Medieval women often had to choose between marrying young, which would mean bearing many children and being in charge of the household, or "taking the veil" and becoming a nun. Many women chose to become nuns to lead a somewhat independent life and even to avoid the risk of childbirth, which could be very dangerous back then. Women were granted a relatively large amount of power in the church, where they could be appointed to become abbesses of convents. If they were inclined to science, philosophy, and the pursuit of knowledge, this would be very appealing. While they were expected to run the convent and spend many of their waking hours in meditation and prayer, these nuns also had the time and space for quiet contemplation. For this reason, many women who contributed to medieval intellectual life were nuns and abbesses.

By the late Middle Ages (ca. 1301–1500), the rights of women began to dwindle in Europe. During the late fourteenth and fifteen centuries, women's property rights began to be taken away and laws were put in place that restricted women's work. Women who had been members—or even leaders—of craft guilds were forced to withdraw and experienced a decline in their salaries as compared to men's salaries. Scholars argue that this was because of a change in European society that was less focused on family and domestic responsibilities and more focused on public institutions during the later Renaissance period.

Despite this shift in the Middle Ages that would lead to diminished rights and responsibilities, women continued to make their mark as writers, philosophers, religious mystics, physicians, and inventors. As the influential French writer Christine de Pizan wrote in her poem "The Poem of Joan of Arc" (1429), "But as for us, we've never heard / About a marvel quite so great / For all the heroes who have lived / In history can't measure up / In bravery against the Maid."[1]

HILDEGARD OF BINGEN (1098–1179)

Hildegard of Bingen was born in what is today Germany in 1098 to a wealthy family. Hildegard claimed to have mystical or religious visions from a very young age, and her parents put her under the care of a convent when she was approximately eight years old. While there, she learned to read and write, as well as how to minister to the sick. She also began to write music and had access to the many books available in the nearby monastery's library.

In 1136, at the age of thirty-eight, Hildegard's mentor and friend, Jutta, died. Jutta had been the abbess of the convent, and Hildegard was

Hildegard of Bingen was an accomplished scholar and writer. Her extensive study of botany and the natural world allowed her to invent many homeopathic remedies.

unanimously elected by the other nuns to take on this most powerful position in the convent. Hildegard's first important decision was to separate her convent from the men's monastery. The men and women lived and worked separately but side by side. This often meant that the nuns were under the supervision of the monks. In order to gain some level of independence, Hildegard decided to move the convent to Rupertsberg. However, the abbot would not allow Hiledgard to do this. In protest, Hildegard lay down and refused to move until the abbot allowed her to move the convent. He granted his permission, and she began to build the new monastery in 1150. At the new monastery of Rupertsberg, Hildegard managed fifty women and eventually turned it into one of the largest and most influential monasteries of the region.

Today, Hildegard is recognized as a polymath. She wrote many manuscripts on subjects as vast as theology, medicine, music, and nature. She also wrote plays and poetry. In particular, Hildegard is acknowledged for founding the scientific field of natural history in Germany—she observed and classified many plants and animals according to their physical and medicinal properties. Hildegard used her knowledge of botany to create medicines to treat many ailments and diseases; she documented these in books such as *Physica* and *Causae et Curae.* Her healing abilities were well known and, in *Causae et Curae*, Hildegard documents her knowledge of the human body and of causes and cures for common ailments. She documents important medical technologies such as treating burns, fractures, dislocations, and other wounds.

It is important to note that Hildegard understood human health in regard to humanity's position in the larger natural world. She believed that health was achieved by a balance of forces and humors and that the use of plants, precious stones, and other medicines was beneficial because they balanced out the excesses in the human body.

In addition to her work in medicine and in natural history, Hildegard invented her own language, a modified Latin alphabet called the *Lingua Ignota*, which is Latin for "unknown language." Scholars are not sure why Hildegard invented and used this language, although many believe that she used it as a "universal language" among the nuns of her monastery to build solidarity among them. Others believe that it was a secret language that was devised by Hildegard to pass important information to a select few. Either way, Hildegard's language is the earliest known constructed language in the world.

In recent years, feminist scholars have become more interested in Hildegard of Bingen. Today, many scholars believe that Hildegard often called herself a lowly member of the "weaker sex" in order to take the focus off of her own achievements and to attribute her accomplishments to divine intervention. This made men take Hildegard's work more seriously during a time when women were viewed as less intelligent and capable than men and were rarely listened to. Since the 1970s, Hildegard's musical compositions have also gained in popularity. From 2000 to 2014, at least four albums featuring her music have been released, including a song inspired by Hildegard written and performed by popular folk singer-songwriter Devendra Banhart. Recent films about Hildegard's life include *Vision*, directed by Margarethe von Trotta in 2009, and *The Unruly Mystics: Saint Hildegard* by director Michael M. Conti in 2014.

TROTULA OF SALERNO (UNKNOWN–1097)

Trotula of Salerno, Italy, is often named as the first gynecologist and the first female professor of medicine. Although not much is known about Trotula, scholars believe that she lived during the late eleventh or early twelfth century CE. Some scholars believe that she came from a wealthy family, married a physician named Johannes Platearius, and had two sons.

Trotula is known for her medical writings, in which she advises women on issues regarding fertility and childbirth. In particular, she is known for two new scientific ideas. One is that men, as well as women, could be infertile. The other is that certain pain medications should be used in childbirth to aid the mother. These ideas were revolutionary because of the views European society held of women in the Middle Ages.

Women were viewed as solely responsible for their fertility, so it was a groundbreaking view that men could be infertile, too. Of course, this caused a lot of anger and disbelief. Additionally, based on teachings by the medieval Catholic Church, women were expected to be in constant pain during childbirth as punishment for their supposed "original sin." Thus, for a learned woman like Trotula to advocate using medicines during childbirth was a new and revolutionary idea.

Trotula's scientific experiments and medical knowledge were published in Latin as the *Passionibus Mulierum Curandorum*. This title is roughly translated as "The Diseases of Women." The sixty-three-volume text was hugely influential in medicine for many centuries after its publication; today, it is still considered the definitive premodern medical text on the topic. It was the first book of its kind to give medical advice to male

Ideas about fertility, pregnancy, and childbirth were quite different during the Middle Ages, as compared to today. Trotula's assertion that women could be made comfortable during labor was radical for the time.

doctors about women's bodies in particular, and it expressed complex ideas for the time about women's fertility and childbirth.

In the sixteenth century, a man named Caspar Wolff published some of Trotula's works under a masculine pen name. This began the enduring belief that Trotula was, in fact, a man and not a woman. This was common throughout the ancient and medieval worlds, and it's the reason why it is very difficult for scholars to determine the inventions and ideas of these historic women. Many women, if they were able to gain the experience and education to invent new technologies and have the ability and the money to publish them, often later had their works disputed because of their gender. Today, more than one hundred medieval manuscripts of texts written by Trotula are in existence, although many more were in circulation during the Middle Ages and the Renaissance.

ISABELLA CUNIO (13TH CENTURY)

Isabella Cunio was an Italian woman who, with her twin brother, Alexander, invented woodblock engraving. Woodblock engraving was the precursor to more advanced forms of printing and flourished during the fifteenth and sixteenth centuries. In the late thirteenth century, Alexander and Isabella were two young teenagers living with their family in Ravenna, Italy. According to tradition, sometime between 1285 and 1287 they cut out illustrations and text from blocks of wood, dipped these blocks in ink, and then pressed them onto paper by hand. Together, they composed and printed a book on Alexander the Great, which consisted of a series of illustrations. The illustrations were described and signed by both twins.

Unfortunately, these first wood engravings do not exist today. Some scholars question whether this story was indeed a true history of wood engraving or if it was simply a legend. If, however, the legend is true, then a young woman (and her twin brother) was responsible for one of the most significant technological advances in the medieval world. By the Renaissance, printers mainly used wood engravings for books and illustrations, until the mid-twentieth century.

In the eighteenth century, a Frenchman known as Monsieur Papillon wrote a book about the history of woodblock engraving. While he stated that this form of engraving was already practiced in China, he mentioned that the Cunio twins were the first Europeans to have used the process. Papillon's contemporaries evaluated these claims as credible. Papillon also wrote that he personally saw the book on Alexander the Great that Isabella and Alexander created. He recounted the rest of the twins' lives, stating that, at the age of nineteen,

Alexander was sent on a military campaign as a knight. He was killed in battle, and Isabella was supposedly so grief stricken by her brother's death that she died soon after.

The book that the Cunio twins supposedly created by inventing woodblock engraving was lost in the eighteenth century, according to Papillon, and never recovered. The names of Isabella Cunio and her brother have been lost to history, and it is likely we will never have physical proof that this sixteen-year-old girl invented one of the most important processes in European history.

ALESSANDRA GILIANI (1307–1326)

Alessandra Giliani was another young Italian woman whose discoveries contributed to the medieval world. Believed to have been born in 1307 in the town of San Giovanni in Persiceto, Italy, Giliani died at the age of nineteen from a septic wound. While she was best known as an early anatomist and physician, she performed many experiments that contributed to medieval technology. As a young woman, she became known as the only qualified prosector in Italy during a time when medical knowledge was based almost entirely on the dissection of corpses.

While she spent most of her life as an assistant to Mondino de Luzzi, who is known as the "father of anatomy," she pioneered a new technology to map the circulatory system. Giliani was the first person to inject cadavers with colored liquids in order to trace the path of the circulatory system. In order to do this, she had to first drain the body of blood. The colored liquids that she then injected into the body would harden, allowing her to learn more about the circulatory system. Many scholars state that her experiments and her development of this new technology led directly to a better understanding of the human circulatory system. However, like many of these early women physicians and inventors, none of her original works remain today.

In 2010, the young adult novelist Barbara Quick wrote *The Golden Web*, which tells a story of how the author imagined Alessandra Giliani's life to be. Quick

While anatomy of the human body was still a mystery, Allessandra Giliani created a new way to study the circulatory system.

researched Giliani but could find little information about her life. However, she was intrigued by manuscript illuminations showing a woman assisting Mondino de Luzzi in one of his experiments. According to a librarian Quick spoke to in Bologna, Italy, during her research, it is very likely that records of Alessandra Giliani's life and accomplishments were deliberately destroyed after her death by church officials who viewed her research as a woman to be threatening to the church's teachings. If this is indeed the case, it is also likely that records of Giliani's family were destroyed.

At the end of Barbara Quick's quest for information about Alessandra Giliani's life, she heard of an old urn located in a church in Bologna. Supposedly, this urn is inscribed with the following words:

> In this urn, awaiting the Resurrection, are the mortal remains of Alessandra Giliani, young woman of Persiecto, adept at anatomical demonstrations and unequalled disciple of the most famous doctor, Mondino de' Liuzzi. She died at the age of 19, consumed by her hard work, on the 26th of March, year of our Lord 1326. This plaque was put here by Ottone [Otto] Agenius Lustrulanus, deprived by [the] loss of his better half, his excellent companion who deserved the best.[2]

JACQUELINE FELICE DE ALMANIA (14TH CENTURY)

Jacqueline Felice de Almania was an Italian physician who lived around the early fourteenth century. During the fourteenth and fifteenth centuries, many more restrictions were placed on women than before. In particular, female healers and physicians were persecuted for their medical

During the fourteenth century, women were discouraged from practicing medicine and other healing arts. Some were accused of witchcraft and burned at the stake.

knowledge. Often, women who were midwives or healers were accused of witchcraft, and many were burned at the stake.

Starting in 1322, de Almania was a licensed physician living and practicing in Paris, France. However, that same year, she was put on trial by well-known male physicians who stated that she was practicing medicine unlawfully. At the time, many doctors practiced medicine without a license. Women, in particular, could not be licensed as doctors because it was illegal for them to receive medical training. Scholars today state that de Almania was particularly threatening to male doctors because she only charged her patients a fee if they were cured by her innovative treatments.

As evidence during the trial, de Almania's accusers stated that she had cured more patients than any other physician in Paris at the time and also that she had performed more complex surgeries successfully. Because women were viewed as naturally inferior to men, they concluded that de Almania could not have truthfully performed such complex and skilled medical operations. She was banned from practicing medicine in France and was threatened with excommunication from the Catholic Church if she ever practiced medicine again. The verdict is viewed by modern scholars as a turning point for female scientists, physicians, and inventors in France in the Middle Ages. From this moment until five hundred years later, women were not allowed to practice medicine in France.

Although we often view history as a continual improvement that builds upon the past for greater justice and freedom, this is not always the case. Women, having greater freedoms in the early Middle Ages, became more and more restricted by the fifteenth century. From the period of the Renaissance, women's rights would be restricted even further still.

CHAPTER THREE

TECHNOLOGY IN THE RENAISSANCE AND THE EARLY MODERN PERIOD

The Renaissance, which means "rebirth" in French, was an important period in Europe that began in the city of Florence, Italy, during the early fifteenth century and lasted until the seventeenth century. (The early modern period overlaps with the Renaissance and is normally stated to have lasted from 1500 to 1800.) At the start of the Renaissance, Italian thinkers and writers rediscovered the works of ancient Greek authors, and this new discovery spurred on their intellectual curiosity. According to author Philip Van Ness Myers, "[U]nder the influence of the intellectual revival the men of Western Europe came to think and feel, to look upon life and the outer world, as did the men of ancient Greece and Rome; and this is again to say that they ceased to think and feel as mediaeval men and began to think and feel as modern men."[1]

This new culture of intellectual curiosity would soon spread out of Florence into the rest of Europe, where Europeans proclaimed the dawn of a new humanism, where men stood at the center of the universe instead of God alone, and scientific inquiry and reasoning could be used to solve any question. Soon, this intellectual curiosity, inspired by the ancient Greeks, expressed itself in art, literature, and new developments in science and technology. Galileo Galilei, who invented a new, more powerful telescope with which he could view the night sky, declared that the sun, and not the Earth, was the center of the universe. Leonardo da Vinci would go on to revolutionize both art and science, and his artistic, scientific, and design works are some of the most precious objects we have today, housed in the largest museums in the world.

The question then becomes: "Did women contribute to the Renaissance?" The scholar Joan Kelly addresses this question by stating that, during the early Middle Ages in Europe, most people worked and lived at home as farmers or in towns as merchants. However, as life moved away from agriculture and public institutions, including universities and libraries, popped up, women were left out of this new public life. Suzanne Hull describes what it was like for women living in the Renaissance in this way:

When England was ruled for half a century by Queens but women had almost no legal power; when marriage, a woman's main vocation cost them their personal property rights; when the ideal woman was rarely seen and never heard in public; when the clothes a woman wore were legally dictated by her social class; when almost all school teachers were men ...[2]

Women in the Renaissance struggled to become educated, to live lives other than as wives and mothers, and to have their voices heard. But despite these incredible odds, many women contributed to art, science, and technology during this period. In fact, Renaissance women contributed to the technologies of medicine, astronomy, and alchemy. Their names may not be as well known as their male counterparts, but their contributions were just as great.

In the seventeenth and eighteenth centuries, women across Europe also struggled against these constraints. As these centuries went on, women were increasingly supposed to act properly and according to their sex, which meant that most intellectual or physical endeavors were seen as improper for women to practice. The exception to this was in the new European colonies, such as the British colonies of North America, where women were granted more autonomy because of the harsh life colonists faced in this new, unfamiliar land. The British laws used in these early American colonies, though, still did not allow women to hold patents in their own names, to operate their own businesses, or to own property.

ISABELLA CORTESE (16TH CENTURY)

Isabella Cortese was a well-known Italian alchemist and writer around the middle of the sixteenth century. Most of her contemporary reputation rests largely on her book, entitled *The Secrets of Lady Cortese*. This book included all of Cortese's knowledge after thirty years spent studying alchemy and medical remedies. First published in Venice, this book includes alchemical recipes to turn metal into gold, as well as other "magical" recipes for things like toothpaste, perfume, glue, soap, and a variety of cosmetics for women. Cortese experimented with chemistry and created such inventions as a "universal medicine" made up of, among other things, camphor, quicksilver, and sulfur. These chemical mixtures functioned on two different levels: at one level, they were supposed to balance mind, body, and soul through magical means; however, these chemical compounds also functioned on a basic medical level, providing relief for such ailments as surface wounds, coughs, or even body odor.

The alchemist Isabella Cortese experimented with magical potions and medical remedies. Her how-to book stirred up the interest of well-to-do women on their trips to the apothecary.

The Secrets of Lady Cortese was immensely popular during the Renaissance. Between 1561, when it was first published, and 1677, eleven editions of the book were published. Translations of the original, such as into German, were also commissioned during this period. Scholars believe that the popularity of the book was due to Cortese's business and marketing sense. She marketed the book to upper-class women as a book of secrets, which would allow them to attain a level of knowledge in alchemy and magic. Cortese maintained the secretiveness of her book by telling her readers that they must keep the secrets in the book to themselves and not talk to others about it. In addition, after they had finished the book, they were encouraged to burn it. The book was reprinted in 1995 and 1996 and is available to modern readers. Currently, the original version of the book is housed in the Marciana National Library in Venice.

In a letter to her brother, Isabella Cortese laid out her rules to become a successful alchemist. She states:

> The first rule is to never work with a Grand Master, but do good work and your life will not have a bad end ... The Second thing you can do is ensure these vessels are strong and well-made, in order not to lose our work through weak vessels and weak medicine. Third, is that you learn to use all the proper materials and metals, and not filter anything because this makes a difference. The fourth is that you not heat too much or too little, but just enough so that nothing fails.[3]

Cortese also advised alchemists to pretend to not know alchemy and to never speak about alchemical secrets, which could risk lessening their skills. The most important rule, according to Cortese, was "that once your work is done, serve God in his glory and give alms to the poor, and pray that you observe these rules so that you will have no troubles."[4]

SOPHIA BRAHE (1556–1643)

Sophia Brahe, the sister of the famous astronomer Tycho Brahe, was an important astronomer and scientist in her own right. In 1573, when she was only seventeen years old, she began to help her twenty-seven-year-old brother, Tycho, with his astronomical observations. Tycho helped educate his younger sister not only in astronomy but in chemistry and horticulture, writing how he was impressed with her "determined mind."

Together, Sophia and Tycho produced the most accurate charts of planetary positions known at that time. But Sophia Brahe also accomplished many other feats. After the death of her first husband, she managed his estate and quickly grew it to great profit. She created a laboratory in her garden and experimented with growing different plants and creating medicines. In particular, Brahe was interested in developing Paracelsian medicines. Paracelsianism was an important movement in the late sixteenth and seventeenth centuries. It followed the theories of the German alchemist Paracelsus in that the activities of the human body were largely chemical and, thus, medicines could be created to balance these chemical reactions. This movement led to great strides in pharmaceutics and developed the chemical basis for many medicines now used today. In particular, Sophia Brahe was interested in the potential use of small doses of poisons to halt the progress of certain diseases.

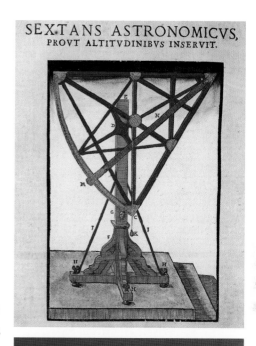

SEXTANS ASTRONOMICVS,
PROVT ALTITVDINIBVS INSERVIT.

Sophia Brahe worked alongside her brother Tycho, who published a book detailing astronomical instruments.

Sophia Brahe also suffered for her interest in science. Her family, an aristocratic and wealthy Danish family who believed that it was improper for their daughter to study medicine, disinherited Sophia. After the death of her second husband, she lived in extreme poverty for many years. During her later years, Brahe moved back to Denmark after having lived most of her life in Sweden and Germany and began work on a monumental nine-hundred-page study of Danish genealogy. Published in 1626, this work, which documents sixty Danish families, is still used today by scholars studying Danish genealogy. Sophia Brahe died in Helsinøgor, Denmark, in 1643 at the age of eighty-seven.

SYBILLA MASTERS (CA. 1670–1720)

Sybilla Masters is often referred to as the first American female inventor. Not much is known about her life prior to 1692, when she was recorded as living in the New Jersey colony. Shortly after this, she married a Quaker merchant and, together, they moved to Philadelphia. Her husband, Thomas Masters, later became a Philadelphia Supreme Court justice and mayor of Philadelphia for two terms.

During this time in the American colonies, life was difficult—especially for women. People depended on the availability of food to feed themselves and their families, and if there was a difficult winter or food shortages, this could cause families to starve. At this time, women were the ones who were expected to prepare food for their families. But this required not only having enough food, but hard physical labor to prepare it without the kitchen appliances we have today.

In the US colonies corn was plentiful, so many households ate corn products like hominy and ground it into a type of cornmeal using two large stones called millstones. This required a lot of physical strength and time. Masters observed Native American women grinding corn in a different way, using wooden posts instead of stones. This gave her the idea to create a mill that used hammers instead of stones or wheels to grind the corn. The resulting corn meal would be automated by a great wheel connected to a hammer used to crush the kernels. Masters's idea would eventually be used to process many different corn and grain products. It changed the colonial economy.

In order to protect her idea, Sybilla Masters wanted to patent her invention. At the same time, she had the idea for a process to weave palm fronds together in order to make hats. She wanted to protect this invention, too. In 1712, she decided to travel to England to get a patent from King George. Not receiving an answer right away, she decided to stay in London and open a shop where she sold the hats she created using her new technique. Finally, in 1715, King George granted her patent for "Cleaning and Curing Indian Corn Growing in the Several Colonies in America."[5] Because patents could not be in a woman's name, it was under the name of Sybilla's husband, Thomas, although it was noted that the idea had been Sybilla's. This was the first patent issued by the king to an American colonist.

The Straw Hat Maker.

Sybilla Masters's patent made improvements to the weaving of straw hats. The savvy businesswoman's inventions boosted the economy of the American colonies.

Then, in 1716, Sybilla Masters's second patent was granted by King George. This was named "Working and Weaving in a New Method, Palmetto Chip and Straw for Hats and Bonnets and Other Improvements of that Ware."[6] For four years, she had been away from her husband and her children in order to receive these patents. Finally, she was able to return home. Together with her husband, she opened up a corn mill and started producing large quantities of what they called Tuscarora Rice, to great success. Sybilla Masters was able to turn her inventions into profitable business deals and changed the economy of the American colonies. While Masters was the first woman to receive a patent in colonial America, she was also the last—at least, until 1793, when the first American patent house was opened.

ANNA MORANDI (1714–1774)

Anna Morandi was born in Bologna, Italy, in 1714. Bologna was an important city for natural science then, and it is home to one of the world's oldest universities. While little is known about Morandi's early life, scholars know that she was well educated, was from a wealthy family, and had professional training as an artist. In 1736, she married a professor of anatomy named Giovanni Manzolini.

During Morandi's time, little was known about the human body. Scientists who wanted to learn more about anatomy used the bodies of poor people who had recently died and dissected them in order to map the human anatomy. Together, the couple dissected more than a thousand bodies in their home. Then, Morandi would complete a wax model of each body. Morandi and Manzolini would then lecture students in anatomy about the growing field, using the wax models in their lectures.

They were so successful that their home competed with established universities in Bologna. In fact, Morandi and Manzolini's work was more accurate than other early work done by anatomists. This was because the wax models that Morandi made allowed students to view anatomy with more precision than they would be able to do on corpses.

In 1755, Manzolini died of tuberculosis, leaving Morandi alone to support herself and their two children. Surprisingly, Morandi took over her husband's position at the University of Bologna and continued to give lectures both at the university and at her home. She even established an anatomical laboratory and gained so much fame that she was invited to Catherine the Great's court in Russia to lecture on her knowledge of anatomy. While the husband and wife worked and published together as a team, after his passing, Morandi is said to have surpassed him in skill and accomplishments. Her wax models were so accurate and close to life that it was often difficult for students to distinguish them from real bodies.

Her work led her to discover previously unknown parts of the human body, including a section of the eye muscle. She is also distinguished for being the first person to ever replicate the tiniest parts

The wax figures made by anatomist and craftswoman Anna Morandi were superior learning tools compared to corpses.

of a human body with stunning accuracy, including capillaries and nerves. One of Morandi's best-known pieces shows her boldness and her skill. It is a life-size self-portrait in wax, depicting Morandi dressed elegantly while poised above a human brain.

NICOLE-REINE LEPAUTE (1723–1788)

Nicole-Reine Lepaute was born in Luxembourg Palace in Paris in 1723. Her father worked as a valet for Louise Élisabeth D'Orléans, the queen of Spain. In 1749, Nicole-Reine married Jean-Andre Lepaute, who worked as the royal clockmaker in the court. Together, they worked on a new clock with an astronomical function. They presented their new invention to the French Academy of Science in 1753, where the couple was commended for their work. After this, Jean-Andre began to construct more astronomical clocks, and he published a text on this in 1755, which included mathematical work done by Nicole-Reine to calculate the oscillations of the pendulums inside the clocks.

Jérôme Lalande, a French astronomer, recognized Nicole-Reine Lepaute's mathematical contributions to creating these astronomical clocks. He recommended her, along with the astronomer Alexis Clairaut, to calculate the predicted return of Halley's comet. Halley's comet had been recorded for thousands of years, but no one knew if its return could be predicted with accuracy. It had been recorded in 1305, 1380, 1456, 1531, 1607, and 1682. In 1705, Edmund Halley, an English astronomer, had stated that this was the same comet that had been seen throughout history and stated that he believed, based on its orbit, that it would return in 1758. Halley died before he could see the comet or further predict when the comet would appear.

Together, Clairaut and Lepaute calculated that Halley's comet would reach perihelion, or the point in the comet's orbit when it was closest to the sun, by mid April 1759. They were incredibly accurate in their calculations as the comet actually reached perihelion on April 13, 1759. This was an incredible astronomical feat. However, Clairaut refused to acknowledge Lepaute's contribution to their calculations when he published the work in 1760. Lalande was furious with Clairaut. When he published a text on their work, he made sure to include Lepaute's name and to properly credit her for her mathematical contributions.

In 1759, Lalande became the editor of a popular astronomical almanac named *Connaissance des temps*. For the sixteen years he was editor, Lepaute contributed to the astronomical tables that were published for each annual issue. She also was known for working alone on the computations for the positions of the sun, the moon, and the planets and for publishing her observations of the transit of Venus across the sun in 1761.

Nicole-Reine Lepaute was a renowned astronomer best known for her contribution to the calculation of Halley's comet's recurrence.

Lepaute continued to contribute to the field of astronomy throughout her life and was eventually elected to the Académie de Béziers, a prestigious society of accomplished philosophers and scientists. She was one of few women to ever hold this honor. While she is recognized for many of her contributions to the field of astronomy today, scholars also understand that many of her contributions may have been lost to time because of her gender. Clairaut's refusal to credit Lepaute for her work because she was a woman was not uncommon at the time, and scientific contributions normally attributed to men may have been because people failed to credit women's work.

CHAPTER FOUR

WOMEN INVENTORS IN THE LONG NINETEENTH CENTURY

The long nineteenth century is a time period that spans from the French Revolution in 1789 until World War I, which lasted from 1914 until 1918. During this time, the Industrial Revolution began in Great Britain and spread around the globe. New inventions, such as an improved efficiency steam engine, the cotton gin, gas lighting, machine tools, and factories, revolutionized the way people worked. Before the Industrial Revolution at the end of the eighteenth century, the global economy was largely built on agriculture; after the Industrial Revolution, it would be based upon manufacturing. This revolution would not have taken place if not for the inventions developed during this time, many of which were designed or aided by women.

The Industrial Revolution also greatly contributed to a change in the way that women lived their lives, as well as in the rights they enjoyed. Following the early modern period, women's rights were gradually restricted. This continued in the nineteenth century mainly because manufacturing became a realm largely controlled by men. As work was moved from the farms to the factories, women were forced to stay at home more and to be relegated to so-called domestic duties of the house, such as cleaning, cooking, and childrearing. In the upper classes in Europe, women were raised and educated for the purpose of making a good economic marriage and bearing children. Any more rigorous education in mathematics, science, and philosophy was discouraged. Depending on their situation, women in the lower classes could be forced to work long hours in factories, where they often worked as textile, or fabric, workers or seamstresses. Women who had to work in factories to earn enough for their families to live on often were still responsible for the bulk of housework and child care. On top of this, men often were given supervisory roles over women workers and, thus, women earned much less than men for the same hours worked.

In the realm of politics, women also faced a grim reality: they were not allowed to vote, not allowed to own property, and had no rights in their marriage. They could not ask for a divorce, nor did they have any rights over their own children.

The Industrial Revolution brought change to the lives of many women. Those who worked in factories and mills were subjected to long hours at low pay.

Despite these formidable odds, women inventors contributed to both the Industrial Revolution and to the new and exciting field of computer science. By the late 1800s, women were organizing and demanding their rights, especially the right to vote. This was called the women's suffrage movement, and these women across Europe and the United States would become known as activists in first-wave feminism.

LADY AUGUSTA ADA BYRON, COUNTESS OF LOVELACE (1815–1852)

Ada Byron was the daughter of the famous Romantic poet Lord Byron and Anne Isabelle Milbanke. Born in 1815, Ada was raised by her mother after her father left England. She received training in mathematics and the sciences and, as a young girl, had already developed sketches and plans for a "flying machine."

Because Ada and her mother traveled in aristocratic circles, she was able to meet other well-know thinkers and scientists. In 1833, when she was just seventeen, Ada met and began a life-long friendship with Charles Babbage, who was a professor of mathematics at Cambridge. Babbage was an important mathematician and inventor who had created something he called the Difference Engine, which was an early calculating machine.

Babbage and Ada often wrote to each other, trading information on mathematics and logic, among other subjects, and Babbage would prove to be an influential figure in Ada's life. Babbage described her as "that Enchantress who has thrown her magical spell around the most abstract of Sciences and has grasped it with a force which few masculine intellects could have exerted over it."[1]

In 1835, Lovelace married William King, who would later inherit the noble title of earl of Lovelace. Ada Byron then became known as the countess of Lovelace. Together, the couple would have three children.

Babbage had plans to make another machine, called the Analytical Engine. Unlike the earlier Difference Engine, the Analytical Engine would not just compute numbers automatically, but would be programmable through the use of punch cards. It had a "store," which was where results would be held, and a "mill," which could perform multiple arithmetical functions. In many ways, it operated like an early computer.

Although Babbage had the original plans to make this machine,

Ada Lovelace had the creative imagination of her father, renowned poet Lord Byron, combined with a scientific pragmatism. The combination served her well.

Lovelace is credited with not only publishing the first detailed plans, but also developing computer programs for this machine and foreseeing the potential use of computers. Due to this publication, called "Sketch of the Analytical Engine, with Notes from the Translator," she is known as the first computer programmer. Babbage never actually made the Analytical Engine, but Alan Turing, who built the first modern computer in the 1940s, based his design on Lovelace's plans.

Ada Lovelace died of cancer at the age of thirty-six.

MARGARET E. KNIGHT (1838–1914)

Margaret E. Knight is known as one of the most famous American female inventors of the twentieth century. However, while her inventions are familiar to many people today, her name has largely been forgotten. Born in 1838 in York, Maine, Knight lost her father, James, at an early age. In order to help support her mother, Knight began working in a cotton mill with her brothers at the age of twelve.

She received little formal education but was precocious from a young age. Some scholars state that at the age of twelve, she had already invented a safety device for powered looms in textile mills.

When she was thirty, she invented a machine that folded and glued the flat-bottomed paper bags we use in grocery stores today. Before this, bags were flat and did not have a wide bottom. Knight thought that she could make bags more useful and, indeed, this invention allowed the mass production of bags that could store many more objects than unfolded bags could. Knight began to build the prototype so that she could apply for a patent; however, a man at the factory where her machine was being built stole her idea and applied for the patent in his own name. Fortunately, Knight filed a lawsuit against him and won; she was awarded her rightful patent in 1871. After this, she opened the Eastern Paper Bag Company in Springfield, Massachusetts, which became an incredibly profitable business.

Later, the very prolific Knight received at least twenty-six more patents for her inventions, most of which involved heavy machinery. In the 1880s, Knight worked on a machine to aid in shoe manufacturing. In the 1900s, after the automobile was invented, Knight invented and received patents for several rotary engines. She passed away at the age of seventy-six in 1914. Margaret E. Knight was inducted posthumously into the National Inventors Hall of Fame in 2006.

MARIE CURIE (1867–1934)

Born Maria Salomea Sklodowska in Warsaw, Poland, in 1867, Marie Curie would go on to become not only one of the most famous women in science, but one of the most famous scientists in history. Curie stood out as a young child for her aptitude in science and her extraordinary memory. Her father, a mathematics and physics teacher, taught his daughter to love math and science. However, when the family lost most of its savings in a bad investment, Curie was forced, while still a teenager, to work in order to earn money for her family. At the age of seventeen, Curie began teaching; she also began to work at a secret "free university," which focused on educating poor Polish women.

In 1891, Curie traveled to Paris to continue her studies in physics at the Sorbonne. By 1894, she began to work in the laboratory of the scientist Gabriel Lippman, who would go on to win the Nobel Prize in Physics. While at the Sorbonne, she met Pierre Curie, who was a professor in physics. They married in 1895, and their marriage would go on to have important historical and scientific significance.

Together, Pierre and Marie Curie worked to investigate radioactivity, which refers to the instability of an atom, causing it to emit radiation.

Marie Curie's experiments with radioactivity earned her the Nobel Prize in Physics in 1903. She was the first woman to win the prize. Remarkably, she was awarded a second Nobel—this time in chemistry—in 1911.

In 1898, Pierre and Marie Curie discovered a new chemical element, polonium, which Marie Curie named after her home country. Shortly thereafter, they discovered radium. These new elements were incredibly radioactive, which meant that they were dangerous to work with. For their work, the Curies, along with scientist Antoine Henri Becquerel, were awarded the Nobel Prize in Physics in 1903.

Marie Curie spent much of her time trying to research pure radium in its metallic state. This formed the basis of her research for which she received her doctorate in 1903, the same year she won the Nobel Prize.

In 1906, Marie Curie was devastated when Pierre was killed in a carriage accident. Despite her grief, she took on Pierre's teaching post at the Sorbonne, becoming the first woman to teach at the famous French university. In 1910, she published on radioactivity, which would become the fundamental text on the subject. In 1911, she received her second Nobel Prize, in chemistry.

During World War I, Marie Curie turned her scientific research to creating X-rays for medical use. She outfitted ambulances with X-rays and even drove them herself to the front line to aid injured soldiers. Despite Curie's many contributions to science, she struggled financially for most of her life. Marie Curie died in 1934 from leukemia, which was caused by exposure to radiation during her research. Pierre and Marie Curie's eldest daughter, Irene, also contributed to the field of chemistry and was awarded a Nobel Prize in Chemistry.

Today, Marie Curie is regarded as one of the greatest scientists who ever lived. And, if you walk through the areas of Paris where she lived and worked, you will find many streets, monuments, and buildings named after her.

MARY ANDERSON (1866–1953)

Born in 1866 in Alabama, Mary Anderson lived many different lives. In 1889, she moved with her mother and her sister to Birmingham, Alabama, which was enjoying a period of development following the destruction caused during the US Civil War. There, she had apartments built and she worked as a real estate developer. Several years later, she moved to Fresno, California, where she operated a cattle ranch for several years before returning to Alabama.

But Anderson's greatest fame grew out of a winter visit to New York City in 1902. While on the snowy streets, she observed that trolley cars were not able to operate efficiently or safely because of snow that fell on the cars' windshields. Anderson sketched out an image of what would later be called windshield wipers in her notebook and, when she returned home to Alabama, she hired a local company to build the device.

Anderson's invention was hand-powered through a lever on the inside of the car, which operated a single rubber arm that moved back and forth across the windshield. While other similar inventions had been proposed, Anderson's was the first model to be effective and to be available to consumers.

The windshield wiper, so essential to the safety and efficiency of motorists today, was invented and patented by Mary Anderson in 1903.

Anderson received a seventeen-year patent for her invention in 1903, but she had difficulty finding companies to market and sell it. However, as the automobile began to gain in popularity, her invention began to sell. In 1922, Cadillac became the first car company to use Anderson's windshield wipers on every car that it manufactured. Of course, windshield wipers are standard on all cars today—although they are no longer operated by hand!

Mary Anderson lived in Birmingham for the rest of her life, where she remained the owner and landlord of the apartments she had built as a young woman. She died in 1953, at the age of eighty-six.

HENRIETTA SWAN LEAVITT (1868–1921)

Henrietta Swan Leavitt was born in Lancaster, Massachusetts, in 1868. She attended Oberlin College and graduated from the Society for the Collegiate Instruction for Women (now known as Radcliffe College) in 1892. After graduating from college, Leavitt continued to take astronomy classes for another year because of her interest in the field. In 1895, she became a volunteer research assistant for the astronomer Edward Pickering at Harvard University. Seven years later, Leavitt was hired on to be a permanent staff member, making thirty cents an hour.

Many women worked in astronomical labs, such as Pickering's at Harvard University, during this time. They were often used as "human computers," categorizing stars and making calculations. These women were rarely ever allowed to take on more theoretical work. For most of Leavitt's time as an assistant, her job was to study photographs of stars and catalogue so-called variable stars, whose brightness changed predictably.

Although astronomer Henrietta Leavitt went largely unheralded during her lifetime, her groundbreaking work influenced many other astronomers, leading to the establishment of our expanding universe.

However, while doing this categorizing in 1912, Leavitt discovered that there was a particular kind of star, which she called a Cepheid variable star, that was brighter if it had a long period of pulsation and dimmer if it had a shorter period of pulsation. Leavitt correctly guessed that these stars, since they were all in the Magellanic Clouds, were at the same relative distance to us. She thus formulated a period-luminosity relationship with Cepheid variable stars, which would allow astronomers to calculate the distance from these stars to Earth based on their period of pulsation and luminosity.

This was an incredibly important moment in the history of astronomy. Because of Leavitt's discovery, later astronomers were able to map our galaxy and, later, our universe. In 1924, Edwin Hubble used Leavitt's research to establish that Cepheid variable stars in the Andromeda nebula could not be within our own Milky Way galaxy because of their distance from us. With this one discovery, astronomers understood for the first time that our Milky Way galaxy was not the only galaxy in the universe and that, instead, the universe is filled with millions and millions of galaxies. Eventually, Hubble would continue his research involving Cepheid variable stars to determine that our universe was, in fact, expanding—which would lead later astronomers to theorize the big bang!

All of this was because of Leavitt's study of Cepheid variable stars. Unfortunately, Leavitt was not recognized for her important work during her lifetime. Pickering continued to treat Leavitt as a lowly assistant in his lab and refused to recognize her for her work. It is often stated that she was a contender for the Nobel Prize—and would likely have won this most prestigious award—if she hadn't died of cancer in 1921. A crater on the moon and an asteroid are named after Leavitt in recognition of her contributions to astronomy.

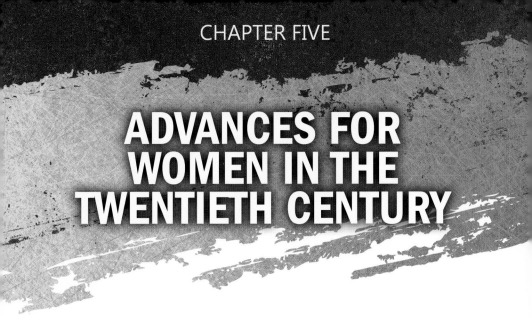

CHAPTER FIVE

ADVANCES FOR WOMEN IN THE TWENTIETH CENTURY

The twentieth century was a time of great change for women in Europe and the United States. In the United States, women gained the right to vote in 1920 with the passage of the Nineteenth Amendment to the US Constitution, which stated that no one could be denied the right to vote based on sex. The Representation of the People Act of 1928 granted women in the United Kingdom equal voting rights to men. In other parts of Europe, women would have to wait several more decades for the right to vote In France, for instance, women were only granted the right to vote in 1944, and in Switzerland the referendum on women's suffrage came as late as 1959.

But this was an exciting time for women. Women's suffrage had been the call of first-wave feminism, which lasted in the United States until 1920. In the early 1960s, second-wave feminism

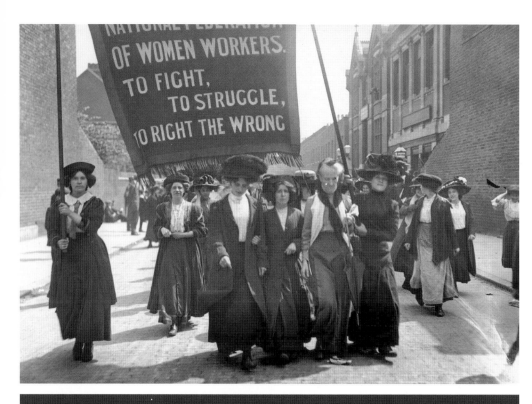

The first-wave feminists in England and the United States fought for basic rights for women, including the crucial right to vote. A second women's rights movement occurred in the 1960s.

began, which broadened women's fight for equal rights in voting and political representation, to greater rights in marriage, reproductive rights, and rights in the workplace. In the 1950s and early 1960s, American women were not admitted to many universities because it was deemed inappropriate for women to seek careers or intellectual pursuits instead of focusing on marriage and children.

The 1960s, however, ushered in great changes in how women were treated in society. Gradually, women were accepted into universities and took on larger roles in business and academics. Often, they made important contributions to technology in the twentieth century but also had to pass formidable obstacles, like being the first in their universities to graduate with advanced degrees in mathematics or physics. These women beat the odds and paved the way for the women who would later hold leadership roles and revolutionize modern science and technology.

MARIA TELKES (1900–1995)

Maria Telkes was born in Budapest, in modern-day Hungary, in 1900. She studied chemistry at the University of Budapest, where she graduated with a PhD in 1924. Soon after she graduated, she moved to the United States, where she began to work as a biophysicist for the Cleveland Clinic Foundation. During her time at the Cleveland Clinic Foundation, Telkes worked with George Crile and, together, they invented a device that could record brain waves.

In 1937, Telkes became a research engineer at Westinghouse Electric. There, she worked on converting heat into electrical energy. Two years later, while at the Massachusetts Institute of Technology

(MIT), she began her first forays into solar energy and solar panels. During World War II, she was commissioned by the navy to develop a solar-powered device that would vaporize salt water and recondense it into drinkable water. This was incredibly important because, during shipwrecks or battles, seamen could be left without water to drink. Eventually, all life rafts were outfitted with this device.

After the war, Telkes continued to investigate solar energy and solar-powered devices. In 1948, Telkes built the first modern solar-powered house with the help of American architect Eleanor Raymond. It was built with boxlike solar collectors that captured the sunlight, warmed the air, and then distributed the warm air around the inside of the house. In order to store this solar energy, Telkes used molten salts such as sodium sulfate, also known as Glauber's salt.

Telkes was widely recognized as an expert in solar energy storage through phase-changing salts, which can effectively hold onto heat during its phase change from solid to liquid until it is later released. For this, Telkes was known as the "sun queen." In 1953, Telkes was awarded a $45,000 grand from the Ford Foundation to build a solar-powered oven. That year, she also invented the first thermoelectric refrigerator.

Maria Telkes is shown adjusting the energy levels in the solar-powered home she helped design. Telkes was a pioneer in the field of solar energy.

Maria Telkes died in 1995, at the age of ninety-four. In 2012, she was inducted posthumously into the National Inventors Hall of Fame.

GRACE HOPPER (1906–1992)

Grace Hopper was born Grace Brewster Murray in New York City in 1906. In 1929, she graduated from Vassar College with a bachelor's degree in math. She continued her studies in math at Yale University, where she received a masters and a doctorate degree. It was a rare feat for a woman to receive a doctorate in mathematics at that time. Only 1,279 women received PhDs in math in the more than seventy years between 1862 and 1934.

In 1930, Hopper married Vincent Foster Hopper. She secured a job as a professor at Vassar and stayed there until 1943. However, when the United States entered World War II, Hopper wanted to contribute to the war effort. In 1943, she joined the United States Naval Reserve. She required a special exemption to enlist because she weighed 15 pounds (7 kilograms) less than the minimum requirement of 120 pounds (54 kg)! In 1945, Vincent and Grace divorced; he was killed later that year while serving in the war.

Because of Hopper's expertise in mathematics, she was assigned to the Bureau of Ships Computation team at Harvard University in

Cambridge, Massachusetts. Under the direction of Howard Aiken, Hopper and her colleagues were tasked with creating the first programmable digital computer. Aiken had proposed the idea for the computer, which he would call the Mark I, in

Grace Hopper works on an early computer called a manual tape punch. Hopper's influence remains today, with the Grace Hopper Celebration of Women in Computing conferences that support the achievements of women in computing.

1937. It was based, in part, on Charles Babbage and Ada Lovelace's work on the Analytical Engine. According to Aiken, the Mark I would bring "Babbage's principles of the Analytical Engine almost to full realization, while adding important new features." Mark I was a mechanical computing machine that would be improved upon in subsequent models by Aiken, Hopper, and their colleagues. During the war, the US Navy used Mark I to compute missile trajectories.

While Hopper had no knowledge of computers before joining the laboratory at Harvard, she quickly became an important member of the team. Following World War II, she remained in the navy and continued on at Harvard, where she helped to develop subsequent models of the Mark computer. While working on the Mark II, Hopper discovered that a moth inside the computer's electrical system was causing it to malfunction. She removed the bug and, thus, invented the terms "bug" and "debug" for computers!

In 1949, Hopper became senior mathematician at the Eckert-Mauchly Computer Corporation. The corporation, headed by J. Presper Eckert and John Mauchly, had built the Electronic Numerical Integrator and Computer (ENIAC), which was the first electronic general-purpose computer. In 1951, the corporation developed UNIVAC, which was an acronym for Universal Automatic

Computer. The UNIVAC would become the first commercially available general-purpose computer in the United States. This early computer weighed 16,000 pounds (7,257 kg) and used 5,000 vacuum tubes to transmit and control electronic signals. The UNIVAC was able to perform approximately one thousand calculations per second. It gained fame during the 1952 presidential election when it predicted Dwight D. Eisenhower would win by a landslide, even though most commentators believed that his rival, Adlai Stevenson, would win.

From 1952 to 1964, Grace Hopper stayed at the Eckert-Mauchly Computer Corporation and worked on a programing language later called FLOW-MATIC to use with the UNIVAC computer. Hopper believed that computer programs should be written in English to make computers more useful for regular consumers and business owners. Because many business owners were interested in using computers to aid with calculating payroll and automatic billing, Hopper believed that the UNIVAC would only be of use to them if it could be programmable in English. However, many of Hopper's colleagues disagreed with her. They told her that it would be impossible to make a computer understand English. By 1952, however, Hopper and her team had developed FLOW-MATIC and had programmed the UNIVAC to understand twenty English commands.

In 1959, Hopper and others used FLOW-MATIC as the basis to develop the programming language COBOL, which stands for common business-oriented language. Today, COBOL remains an important English-like computer programming language used in the business, finance, and administrative sectors. Hopper strongly believed that there should be an international standardization of computer languages, and she often advocated for this publicly.

Grace Hopper was not only a brilliant early computer scientist; she also had the charisma and the business sense to popularize her work in order to get business owners to adopt it. Hopper had the technical skills to create FLOW-MATIC and COBOL, but she also had the speaking skills and marketing savvy to help others to understand their use, too. This, in some way, was just as important as her technical work; without Hopper's great speaking ability, businesses may never have adopted the computer language that she believed so fervently would improve the way people conducted business around the world.

Hopper retired from the navy in 1966; however the navy soon called her back to duty and asked for her services "indefinitely." In 1973, Hopper was promoted to captain, and in 1977 she became special adviser to the commander of the Naval Data Automation Command. In 1986, Hopper retired from the navy permanently; at eighty years old, she was the oldest active duty officer in the United States military.

In 1985, she was promoted to rear admiral and received the Defense Distinguished Service Medal, the highest award granted by the Department of Defense. Throughout her career, Hopper was given numerous awards for her work, including thirty-seven honorary degrees between 1972 and 1987. Hopper was also awarded the National Medal of Technology in 1991—the first individual woman to ever receive the United States' highest technology award. Grace Hopper died in 1992, at the age of eighty-five.

HEDY LAMARR (1914–2000)

Hedy Lamarr was not just a famous Hollywood actress but also a pioneer in early wireless communications. Born in 1914 in Vienna (then Austria-Hungary) Lamarr was discovered by a talent scout when she was a young teenager. In the late 1920s, she traveled to Berlin and trained in theater under the mentorship of famous producer Max Reinhardt. In 1933, at the age of eighteen, she starred in her first movie, a German film called *Ecstasy*.

That same year she married her first husband, Friedrich Mandl, an Austrian who had made a fortune selling weapons. In later years, Lamarr described her life with Mandl as unbearable and claimed that he kept her a prisoner in the castle in which they lived. Mandl had ties with the Fascist regime in Italy and with the Nazi government in Germany because of his job selling weapons.

In 1937, Lamarr decided that she must escape; in her autobiography, she wrote that she wore a maid costume to disguise herself and snuck out of her country. She ended up in Paris, where she met Louis B. Mayer, an American film producer and the cofounder of MGM Studios. Soon, Lamarr was starring in Hollywood movies, the first being *Algiers*, which was an instant hit. Audiences were stunned by her beauty, and Lamarr went on to appear in many famous Hollywood movies, including *Boom Town* (1940) with Clark Gable, *Tortilla Flat* (1942), and Cecil B. Demille's *Samson and Delilah* (1949).

While Hedy Lamarr is known for her work in Hollywood—and her beauty— she was also an important and prolific inventor. Following her arrival in the United States, Lamarr wanted to help

Hollywood movie star Hedy Lamarr developed a technology for guiding missiles during World War II.

the Allied war effort against Nazi Germany by creating a "secret communications system." Along with coinventor George Antheil, Lamarr developed a frequency-hopping spread-spectrum system in 1942. This machine could transmit "secret" radio messages by "hopping" rapidly from one radio frequency to the next over irregular periods of time. This would make it very difficult for an enemy to intercept classified messages transmitted in this way.

While the patent was awarded to Antheil and Lamarr, the machine was never actually produced. However, the device was influential in later years, when a similar machine was developed independently and Lamarr and Antheil's patents were rediscovered. During the Cuban missile crisis in 1962, the device was implemented on naval ships for the first time and, since then, it has been used in many military missions.

Lamarr's contribution to spread-spectrum technology, which is really just signals that are spread out over a certain range of frequencies, directly influenced later wireless technology, including the development of cell phones, fax machines, and other wireless devices.

Lamarr was not recognized for her inventions during her lifetime. She died in 2000. In 2014, Lamarr and Antheil were inducted into the National Inventors Hall of Fame.

GIULIANA TESORO (1921–2002)

Throughout her life, Giuliana Tesoro received more than 125 patents. Born in Venice, Italy, in 1921, Giuliana Cavaglieri moved to the United States in 1939 to escape Benito Mussolini's fascist regime. She entered Yale University's graduate program in organic chemistry soon after arriving in the United States and received her PhD there in 1943 when she was just twenty-one years old. That same year she married Victor Tesoro, with whom she had two children.

After receiving her PhD, Tesoro worked at Onyx Oil and Chemical Company in 1944; she was promoted to assistant director of research in 1955 and then to associate director in 1957. With her background in chemistry, she began to do research in textiles. Over the course of the next twenty years, she would develop the first antistatic chemical that could be applied to synthetic fabric and flame-resistant and permanent press, or wrinkle-resistant, fabrics.

She spent several years as a professor at MIT before being appointed research professor at the Polytechnic Institute of New York University in Brooklyn, New York, from 1982 until 1996. She founded the Fiber Society, a group dedicated to advancing the science regarding fibers, and served as its president. She also served on three National Research Council committees on polymeric materials, fire-retardant clothing, and toxic materials. In 1978, she was awarded the Society of Women Engineers' Achievement Award.

Giuliana Tesoro died in Dobbs Ferry, New York, in 2002, at the age of eighty-one.

STEPHANIE LOUISE KWOLEK (1923–2014)

Stephanie Louise Kwolek was born to Polish parents in New Kensington, Pennsylvania, in 1923. Kwolek was always interested in science, which she attributed to her father's work as a naturalist and the many hours they spent exploring nature together during her childhood. In 1946, Kwolek graduated from Margaret Morrison Carnegie College, the women's college of the Carnegie Institute of Technology, with a bachelor's degree in chemistry. Immediately after graduation, she went to work at DuPont, one of the largest chemical companies in the world. Kwolek dreamed of attending medical school and planned to stay at DuPont only long enough to finance her medical education, but she enjoyed what she did there and stayed on for the rest of her career.

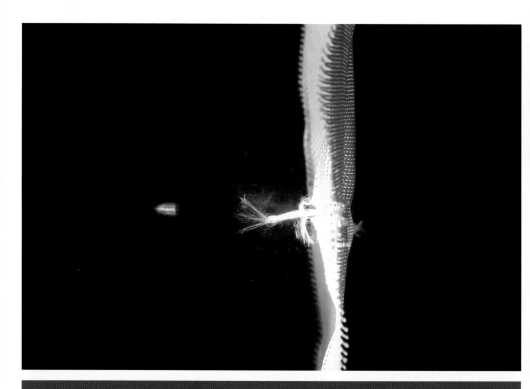

Stephanie Kwolek invented Kevlar almost by accident. The superstrong fiber has been used in a variety of important applications, including military armor, spacecraft, cookware, and tires.

In 1965, Kwolek was part of a team tasked with developing a stronger synthetic fiber. The scientists spent many hours trying to develop this new synthetic fiber, without any luck. Then Kwolek announced that she had created a crystal-like liquid that could be spun into fibers. She had created this by dissolving aramid polyamides into a solvent. At first, her colleagues thought that the liquid was too thin to be strong. But, after Kwolek spun the liquid into fibers, she realized that she had created the strongest fiber ever known. In fact, Kwolek had invented Kevlar, which is five times stronger than steel and much, much lighter. She patented Kevlar in 1966. In an interview in 2007, Kwolek admitted, "I never in a thousand years expected that little liquid crystal to develop into what it did."[1]

Today, Kevlar is best known for forming the basis of body armor that protects military service members, police, and even scientists from gunshots, explosions, and other dangers. But Kevlar is also used in many other ways. It is used for its strength and durability in such items as tires, helmets, kayaks, drums, frying pans, and even spacecraft. It has been used to protect underwater cables and the suspension cables that hold up bridges. Kevlar is an important material that is used in many ways and has protected many thousands of lives.

In 1995, Stephanie Kwolek was the fourth woman to be inducted into the National Inventors Hall of Fame. In 2003, she was inducted into the National Women's Hall of Fame. Kwolek has received many other awards since she invented Kevlar. She retired from DuPont in 1989 and died at the age of ninety in 2014.

ERNA SCHNEIDER HOOVER (1926–)

Erna Schneider Hoover was born in Irvington, New Jersey, in 1926. As a young child, she was interested in science and in Marie Curie. Reading Curie's biography, Hoover realized that as a woman, she, too, could succeed in science.

Hoover attended the all girls Wellesley College and graduated with a bachelor's degree (with honors) in medieval history in 1948. However, Hoover decided to switch her educational focus to going back to graduate school. Attending Yale University, Hoover pursued a doctorate in philosophy and mathematics, graduating in 1951. This was an incredible accomplishment: in the 1940s, only 5 percent of doctoral degrees in mathematics were awarded to women.

At first, Hoover thought that she would become a professor. However, she was unable to find a stable job teaching, perhaps because of her gender. So Hoover decided to become a researcher at Bell Laboratories in 1954. In 1956, Hoover received a promotion at Bell, allowing her to work more on computer programming.

While working in this new position, Hoover realized that, at call centers, the load of telephone calls coming in would put so much pressure on the switchboard that the whole system would shut down. So, while in the hospital after giving birth to her second child, Hoover devised a way to program computers so that they could handle large numbers of incoming calls at once. This became known as stored program control, and it meant that service during peak call times would not be dropped as often.

Hoover applied for a patent for her invention, called the "Feedback Control Monitor for Stored Program Data Processing System," in 1967 and finally received it in November 1971. It was the first software patent ever issued in the United States.

Because of her work, Hoover received a promotion and was one of the first women to oversee a technical department at Bell Labs.

Erna Hoover worked at Bell until retiring in 1987, after thirty-two years of service. She was inducted into the National Inventors Hall of Fame in 2008, and her invention is still an integral part of telecommunications today.

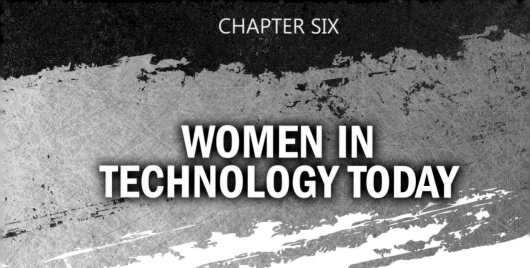

CHAPTER SIX

WOMEN IN TECHNOLOGY TODAY

Today, women are the CEOs of major corporations, professors, and computer programmers, and they continue to pioneer in the fields of technology and science. Young girls today will grow up with role models like Grace Hopper and Sheryl Sandberg and are told that their gender does not need to dictate their career paths.

However, despite the female mentors and role models who encourage the younger generations, there are many obstacles that women still face in the workforce. Women in the early twenty-first century continue to be paid less than their male counterparts for the same work. In the United States, there is no federally mandated maternity leave, which means that women often have to choose between staying with their newborns and recovering from childbirth or returning to work immediately.

Some important female leaders in technology, such as Sheryl Sandberg and Marissa Mayer, are criticized for being out of touch with the struggles of middle- and lower-class women when they tell them to focus on their careers even if it means spending less time with their families or outsourcing domestic tasks. While modern men are taking on a greater role in the home, women still disproportionately take on domestic tasks like cleaning, cooking, and raising children. Many women today believe that there are still great strides to be made for gender equality.

But that doesn't mean that we should not celebrate women's accomplishments and the rights that previous generations of female activists fought so hard for. Some of the women in this chapter are among the most powerful and wealthiest people in the world. Their activism for the next generation of women will ensure that women in technology years from now will continue to have even greater opportunities, guaranteeing generations of women leaders and innovators for years to come.

SHIRLEY JACKSON (1946–)

Born in Washington, DC, in 1946, Shirley Jackson was interested in science from a very young age. She graduated as valedictorian of her high school and then, in the mid-1960s, began college at MIT as part of the first cohort of African American students. In her undergraduate class, she was one of only two women. While at MIT, she received her bachelor's degree in science in 1968 and then her PhD in theoretical physics in 1973. Jackson became the first African American woman to receive a PhD in physics from MIT.

After graduating from MIT, she got a job as a research scientist at the Fermi National

In 2015, President Barack Obama awarded the National Medal of Science to Shirley Jackson. The award is the highest honor for scientific achievement recognized by the US government.

Accelerator Laboratory, popularly known as Fermilab. Located in Illinois, Fermilab is a laboratory where scientists can study high-energy particles. Its particle accelerator, a machine that propels charged particles like electrons or photons at near light speeds in order to study what happens when such particles collide, was the world's second largest and formed an underground circle nearly 4 miles (6.4 kilometers) long. During her time at Fermilab, Jackson studied large subatomic particles known as hadrons.

In 1976, Jackson took a job at Bell Laboratories. There, she studied ceramic materials in order to investigate whether these materials could conduct large amounts of electricity. She also conducted research that would greatly influence the field of telecommunications. Jackson's research helped to develop such new technologies as caller ID, fax machines, and call waiting.

President Bill Clinton appointed Jackson the chairwoman of the US Nuclear Regulatory Commission in 1995. This commission is responsible for overseeing safe nuclear energy use in the United States, and Jackson was both the first woman and the first African American to serve as chair.

In 1995, Jackson was appointed president of Rensselaer Polytechnic Institute, where she was also the first woman and first African American to occupy the position. She became known for her work advancing science education at Rensselaer, which is one of the top fifty universities in the United States. She was also the highest paid college president during her term, earning approximately $1.6 million in 2009. In 1998, Jackson was inducted into the National Women's Hall of Fame. She remains president of Rensselaer today and continues to advocate for women in science.

JEAN E. SAMMET (1928–)

Jean Sammet was born in New York City in 1928. Although computers were still in their infancy during Sammet's childhood and young adulthood, she said that she was always interested in the opportunities that computing offered: "From childhood on, I hated to throw papers away. As I became an adult this characteristic merged with my interest in computing history."[1]

Sammet graduated from Mount Holyoke College with a bachelor's degree in mathematics in 1948 and then received her master's in mathematics from the University of Illinois. After receiving her master's degree, Sammet began working at various companies in computer science and programming. At Sperry Gyroscope, a large electronics company based in New York, she created and supervised the first scientific programming

Jean Sammet spent much of her career at IBM developing programming languages. Here, an IBM employee operates a 7044 mainframe computer in 1961.

group. After leaving Sperry Gyroscope in 1958, she began to work for the COBOL group, headed by Grace Hopper, which developed an English-like programming language for the early UNIVAC computer.

In 1961, Sammet was hired by IBM. She moved to Boston, where she managed the IBM Data Systems Division as an advanced programmer. While in this role, Sammet developed FORMAC (a shortening of "Formula Manipulation Compiler"), an early programming language used for algebraic computations. She received an IBM Outstanding Contribution Award for this work in 1965. That same year she published her best-known work, *Programming Languages: History and Fundamentals*. This reference book was the standard text for those who wanted to learn computer programming and programming languages at this time, and it is still considered a classic today.

Sammet continued to develop different programming languages for IBM throughout the 1960s and 1970s, including the Ada programming language. In 1972, Sammet was elected vice president of the Association for Computing Machinery (ACM), the largest computing society in the world. She was elected the first female president of ACM in 1974 and served a two-year term. In 1977, Sammet was elected to the US National Academy of Engineering. Sammet is known as a world authority on the history of computer programming languages, and she continues to win awards today.

FRANCES ALLEN (1932–)

Frances Allen was born on a farm in Peru, New York, in 1932. She received her bachelor's degree in mathematics from Albany State Teachers

College in 1954 and a master's degree in mathematics from the University of Michigan in 1958. Allen planned to teach math and began her teaching career in her hometown of Peru. However, she struggled to pay for her student loans on her minimal salary. Then an opportunity to work at IBM presented itself. While Allen had never thought to work in industry before, she told herself that she would accept the position to pay off her debts and only work there for a few years. However, she ended up loving her job at IBM and stayed on for forty-five years.

In her early years at IBM, Allen's work consisted of training new staff members on a new programming language called FORTRAN. FORTRAN was first created in 1957 by John Backus and was a programming language developed for simplicity and ease of use. Unlike other programming languages, FORTRAN was created through a combination of English shorthand and simple algebraic equations, through which users could communicate with computers.

Throughout the 1960s, Allen continued to work with programming languages and supercomputers at IBM. Supercomputers are extremely powerful high-performance computers that are often used by scientists to perform such tasks as mapping the evolution of the universe or predicting weather patterns, which require complex mathematical computations. In particular, Allen worked on developing compilers for these supercomputers, which are programs that translate a programming language into a different code that the computer can easily analyze and decode.

Allen continued to work at IBM until her retirement in 2002. She was the first woman to be named an IBM fellow in 1989. Allen also has received the Augusta Ada Lovelace Award from the Association of Women in Computing. In 2006, she was the first woman to be named a Turing Award recipient. Her important contributions to the field of computer science were enumerated during this award citation:

> Fran Allen's work has had an enormous impact on compiler research and practice. Both alone and in joint work with John Cocke, she introduced many of the abstractions, algorithms, and implementations that laid the groundwork for automatic program optimization technology ... Allen developed and implemented her methods as part of compilers for the IBM STRETCH-HARVEST and the experimental Advanced Computing System. This work established the feasibility and structure of modern machine- and language-independent optimizers.[2]

RADIA PERLMAN (1951–)

Radia Perlman is often referred to as "the mother of the internet." Born in Portsmouth, Virginia, and raised in New Jersey, Perlman's parents were both engineers, and she grew up interested in using math and technology to solve pressing problems. Perlman enrolled at MIT in 1969, where she took a class in computer programming. The assistant in the class recognized that Perlman was especially gifted and helped her get a job at MIT teaching children basic programming skills while attending the university. As a teacher, Perlman created and programmed a robot named Turtle in the hopes of making programming not only educational, but also fun. Perlman graduated with a bachelor's degree in mathematics in 1973. She also received a master's degree in mathematics in 1976 and a PhD in computer science in 1988 from MIT.

Radia Perlman has made surfing the internet and retrieving information efficient and easy.

Perlman recalls giving a presentation as a software designer in the mid-1970s. At the time, few women were in the field and she gave her presentation to a room full of men. Perlman spent her thirty-minute presentation offering a solution to a common routing problem. However, at the end of her presentation, no one seemed to have paid any attention to what she had said. "At the end of the meeting, the organizers still called for a solution after I had just given them one, which really irked me," Perlman recalls.[3] She felt that it was because she was a woman in a male-dominated field.

Over the course of her career, while working for large computer companies such as Sun Microsystems, Perlman has revolutionized the field of computer science. Her innovations have led to more than a hundred patents, which are held in the names of the companies for which she has worked. Her work has not only helped make the internet more secure, but has helped speed up the transfer of data among network systems.

But what Perlman is best known for is something called the spanning tree algorithm. In other words, Perlman developed software that helps data move from one area to another on the internet. Without her work, it would be difficult to "surf" the internet as we do today, moving easily from one website to another. In fact, her work is solely responsible for the ability to create large networks, which is why she is often referred to as "the mother of the internet."

Throughout her career, Perlman has won numerous awards. Her most recent recognition was being inducted into the Internet Hall of Fame in 2014.

ANITA BORG (1949–2003)

Anita Borg taught herself to program while working in the insurance industry. She was always interested in math but never had the ability to take formal classes. Soon, however, she realized that she must follow her passion. She began work at her first programming job in 1969 and went back to school to pursue a doctorate in computer science, graduating from New York University in 1981 at the age of thirty-two.

In 1986, Borg began to work for Digital Equipment Corporation. While there, she worked on improving high-speed memory systems. Soon, she grew more interested in the possibilities of email communication. In 1987, she founded the influential Systers mailing list, which was designed to help women in computing communicate and advocate for one another. This led Borg to become more interested in communication through virtual communities.

While Borg's technical work was important, it was her advocacy for women in technology that became her passion. According to Brian Reid, who worked with Borg at Digital Equipment, "Somewhere in the middle of doing all this technical research she realized that what she really wanted to do was not study computers but use computers to link people."[4] Borg was one of the first people to recognize not just the technical

Anita Borg was a computer science whiz, but perhaps her greatest contributions were her efforts to connect women in the field. Her innovations helped promote women's excellence in technology and engineering.

uses of the internet, but also its uses as a communication device to virtually connect people around the world.

Borg's Systers mailing list continued to expand, reaching more than 2,500 women across 38 different countries in 2003. While it was originally created by Borg for women with specialized technical training to exchange ideas, it became a platform to advocate for women in engineering and computer science. In 1992, Borg's Systers list was influential in forcing Mattel to remove a microchip from a speaking Barbie doll that said, "Math class is tough."

Borg also cofounded the Grace Hopper Celebration of Women in Computing conference in 1994 with computer scientist Telle Whitney. This conference is held every two years for women in the computing fields. In 1997, she founded the Institute for Women and Technology (IWT), a nonprofit organization that helps to educate, recruit, and aid women interested in technology. Today, the IWT is headed by Telle Whitney and the organization is still an important force in technology for women around the world.

Anita Borg won many awards throughout her lifetime, including the Augusta Ada Lovelace Award in 1995. In 1996, she was inducted into the Association for Computing Machinery. President Bill Clinton appointed Borg to the Presidential

Commission on the Advancement of Women and Minorities in Science, Engineering, and Technology in 1999. That same year, Borg was diagnosed with a brain tumor. She continued to work until 2002 and died in 2003.

SHERYL SANDBERG (1969–)

Sheryl Sandberg has gained worldwide fame, not only for her important position with one of the largest companies in the world, but also for her advocacy for women in technology.

Sandberg was born in Washington, DC, in 1969. She worked hard in school as a young girl and was always one of the top students in her class. In 1987, Sandberg enrolled at Harvard University. She graduated in 1991 with a degree in economics and, two years later, returned to Harvard again to earn an MBA from Harvard Business School.

She followed her mentor, Larry Summers, back to Washington, DC, to work for him while he served as United States secretary of the treasury under the administration of President Bill Clinton. When President Clinton's term was over, Sandberg moved to Silicon Valley— so called because it is the center of technological innovation in the United States—in northern California and began working for Google as vice president of global online sales and operations.

At a 2007 Christmas party, Sandberg had a seren-
dipitous encounter with a young entrepreneur and
programmer named Mark Zuckerberg. Zuckerberg
cofounded Facebook as a student at Harvard in
2003 with Eduardo Savarin, Andrew McCollum,
Dustin Moskovitz, and Chris Hughes. This social
networking site expanded rapidly, becoming the
largest social networking website in the world and
one of the largest companies ever formed. When

Sheryl Sandberg didn't invent Facebook, but she is credited with making it profitable. Since making a name for herself, Sandberg has devoted time to advocating for women, although some accuse her of being out of touch.

Zuckerman met Sandberg, he immediately knew that she would be the perfect fit for his company. He soon asked her if she would work for Facebook as its chief operating officer (COO).

As COO, Sandberg was tasked with making Facebook more profitable. Facebook was a global website, but it didn't have a profit strategy. Sandberg changed this by introducing advertisements to Facebook. Because of her strategy, Facebook became profitable by 2010.

But, in recent years, Sandberg has become as known for her advocacy for women as for her financial prowess in the tech industry. In 2013, she published *Lean In: Women, Work, and the Will to Lead.* This book was written in response to the experiences women shared with Sandberg after she gave a TED talk on "the ways women are held back—and the way we hold ourselves back." The book examines the role of women in the workforce and how women can achieve higher leadership positions in industry. According to Sandberg, women need to "lean in," to stick to their careers even with the pressures of raising children and caretaking. The book immediately became popular, selling more than one million copies in the six months following its publication.

Anne-Marie Slaughter, a professor, lawyer, and political analyst, describes Sandberg's message in this way:

Her point, in a nutshell, is that notwithstanding the many gender biases that still operate all over the workplace, excuses and justifications won't get women anywhere. Instead, believe in yourself, give it your all, "lean in" and "don't leave before you leave"—which is to say, don't doubt your ability to combine work and family and thus edge yourself out of plum assignments before you even have a baby.[5]

Indeed, women who balance careers and family often experience what is known as "the baby penalty." Because the bulk of raising children and taking care of the household still falls more on women than men, women are often penalized in the workforce for having to take on the responsibilities of home and children. Often, women feel discouraged by this and some give up their careers or take a backseat in their companies, which means taking on less responsibilities, not standing for promotions and, thus, not earning as much as men. Sandberg states that there is gender discrimination in the workplace, but that women also need to determine what it is that they want and have the confidence to go for it.

In her book, Sandberg tells an anecdote about Virginia Rometty, who was the first female chief executive officer at IBM. When Rometty was offered a big promotion when she was just beginning her career, she responded that she would have to think about it because she wasn't sure if she had enough experience to take on the position. She spoke to her husband about it that night, who told her: "Do you think a man would ever have answered that question that way?" Rometty accepted the position and often told the story in order to encourage women to have confidence in themselves.

However, while Sandberg's message can be incredibly powerful for women, she has received backlash for her message to women of "leaning in." As Slaughter states, "This is the book of someone who has never met a challenge she couldn't surmount by working harder and believing in herself." Many women, though, state that hard work goes only so far and that women are often penalized for having families even when they do "lean in," and sometimes "leaning in" is not possible without additional resources or support. Slaughter states: "When it comes to ensuring that caregivers still have paths to the corner office, how can business lean in?"[6]

In 2014, Sheryl Sandberg continued her activism through campaigning to ban the word "bossy" because of the way it harms women's perception of themselves. Sandberg continues to campaign for women's rights in the workforce. In 2015, Sandberg's husband, Dave Goldberg, died suddenly from an accident at the age of forty-seven. In raising their daughter as a single mother, Sandberg amended some of the advice she had written in *Lean In*, stating that she hadn't understood the challenges unique to single parents.

MARISSA MAYER (1975–)

Marissa Mayer was born in Wausau, Wisconsin, in 1975. As a child, she was painfully shy. Her family encouraged her to take ballet and piano lessons in part to teach her to become more "confident and poised."

In high school, Mayer excelled in the sciences, including chemistry and biology. She planned to go to medical school and to become a pediatric surgeon. However, while taking classes at Stanford University, she became more and more interested in computer science. She was especially interested in artificial intelligence, or making computers more humanlike. She graduated with a bachelor's degree in 1997 and, in 1999, a master's degree in computer science. For her thesis, she designed a computer program that gave travel recommendations to users using a humanlike voice. She holds several patents in artificial intelligence.

After graduating from Stanford, Mayer was offered many jobs—including teaching computer science at Carnegie Mellon University. However, she chose to work at a new company named Google in 1999 as the company's first female engineer. She wrote code for Google and helped develop such programs as Adwords. In 2005, she became vice president of search products and user experience.

In 2012, Mayer left Google to become president and CEO of Yahoo!. While at Yahoo!, her management style has been both praised and criticized. After giving birth in 2013, she returned to work soon after and kept her son in a nursery she had built next to her office. This was viewed by Mayer's supporters as both a way for women to "have it all" and a way to publicize the role of mothers in the workforce, but she was criticized by her detractors for showing an unrealistic solution that most women could never even hope to have. That same year, Mayer increased maternity leave at Yahoo! and instituted a bonus program for new parents.

In 2014, Mayer was ranked the sixteenth most powerful businesswoman in the world by *Forbes* magazine. She sits on the board of directors of many large tech corporations and is one of the highest-paid women in the world.

CONCLUSION

The United States—and much of the world—still has a long way to go before women achieve full equality in the workforce, especially in the fields of science, math, and technology. However, many great women have paved the way for the next generation of female inventors, engineers, and scientists. In acknowledging the accomplishments of those women who came before us—even if they lived and worked one thousand years ago—we acknowledge that women are capable, and have always been capable, of thinking, creating, and engineering revolutionary technologies that continue to change our world.

CHAPTER NOTES

INTRODUCTION

1. Janelle Brown, "Women Proto-Programmers Get Their Just Reward," *Wired*, May 1997, http://archive.wired.com/culture/lifestyle/news/1997/05/3711 (accessed March 30, 2016).

CHAPTER 1. WOMEN AND TECHNOLOGY IN THE ANCIENT WORLD

1. Margaret Alic, *Hypatia's Heritage: A History of Women in Science from Antiquity Through the Nineteenth Century* (Boston, MA: Beacon Press, 1986), p. 21.
2. Ibid., p.29.
3. Ibid., p.37.
4. Ibid., p.39.
5. Ibid.
6. Ibid.

CHAPTER 2. WOMEN'S INNOVATIONS DURING THE MIDDLE AGES

1. Charity Cannon Willard, *The Writings of Christine de Pizan* (New York, NY: Persea Books, 1994).
2. Barbara Quick, "Alessandra in History," A Golden Web, http://barbaraquick.com/alessandra.html (accessed March 30, 2016).

CHAPTER 3. TECHNOLOGY IN THE RENAISSANCE AND THE EARLY MODERN PERIOD

1. Excerpt from Van Ness Myers, Philip, *Mediaeval and Modern History* (Boston, MA: Ginn and Company, 1905), pp. 251–274, Sam Houston State University, http://www.shsu.edu/~his_ncp/Renn.html (accessed March 30, 2016).
2. Suzanne W. Hull, *Women According to Men: The World of Tudor-Stuart Women* (Walnut Creek, CA: Alta Mira Press, 1996).
3. Gigi, "Alchemy in Renaissance Italy," La Bella Donna: The Italian Renaissance ReLived, February 19, 2013, https://fleurtyherald.wordpress.com/2013/02/19/alchemy-in-renaissance-italy (accessed March 30, 2016).
4. Ibid.
5. Maggie Maclean, "Sybilla Masters," History of American Women, *Women History Blog*, August 2008, http://www.womenhistoryblog.com/2008/08/sybilla-masters.html (accessed March 30, 2016).
6. Ibid.

CHAPTER 4. WOMEN INVENTORS IN THE LONG NINETEENTH CENTURY

1. Sydney Padua, "Who Was Ada Lovelace?" Ada Lovelace Day, http://findingada.com/about/who-was-ada/ (accessed March 30, 2016).

CHAPTER 5. ADVANCES FOR WOMEN IN THE TWENTIETH CENTURY

1. Camila Domonoske, "Stephanie Kwolek, Chemist Who Created Kevlar, Dies at 90," NPR, June 20, 2014, http://www.npr.org/sections/thetwo-way/2014/06/20/323951708/stephanie-kwolek-chemist-who-created-kevlar-dies-at-90 (accessed March 30, 2016).

CHAPTER 6. WOMEN IN TECHNOLOGY TODAY

1. Computer History Museum, "Jean Sammet," http://www.computerhistory.org/fellowawards/hall/bios/Jean,Sammet/(accessed June 5, 2016).
2. ACM A.M. Turing Award, "Frances Alan," Association for Computing Machinery, http://awards.acm.org/award_winners/allen_1012327.cfm (accessed June 5, 2016).
3. Matt McGann, "Radia Perlman '73, Mother of the Internet," MIT Admissions, http://mitadmissions.org/blogs/entry/radia_perlman_73_mother_of_the (accessed March 30, 2016).
4. Katie Hafner, "Anita Borg, 54, Trailblazer for Women in Computer Field," *New York Times,* April 10, 2010, http://www.nytimes.com/2003/04/10/us/anita-borg-54-trailblazer-for-women-in-computer-field.html (accessed March 30, 2016).

5. Anne-Marie Slaughter, "Yes, You Can: Sheryl Sandberg's 'Lean In,'" *New York Times*, March 10, 2013, http://www.nytimes.com/2013/03/10/books/review/sheryl-sandbergs-lean-in.html (accessed March 30, 2016).

6. Ibid.

alloy A mixture that contains metal.

computation A mathematical calculation.

Confucianism Philosophical and ethical teachings developed by the Chinese philosopher Confucius during the fifth century BCE; this philosophy stresses the importance of respect for one's male elders.

Fascist regime A system of government where a dictator holds control of government functions, suppresses personal freedoms, and often promotes racist or nationalist policies.

first-wave feminism A period of activism from the late nineteenth to the early twentieth century where women fought for legal rights, especially the right to vote.

Gnosticism A movement that occurred within the Christian church in the second century that stressed that knowledge could lead humans to redemption.

gynecology The branch of medicine that deals with the physical health of women and girls, particularly the reproductive system.

horticulture The art of garden cultivation and maintenance.

humanism A cultural movement in the Renaissance where artists and philosophers looked to ancient Greek works for inspiration.

luminosity The total amount of energy emitted by a star or galaxy.

misogynism A hatred or distrust of women.

patent The exclusive right over an invention in exchange for public disclosure of the invention, usually granted by governments.

polymath A person who has deep knowledge across many fields.

posthumously After one's death.

precocious Describes someone who shows extraordinary ability at a young age.

prolific Describes someone who is very productive or who creates many things.

prosector An anatomist.

pulsation A rhythmic beating or throbbing.

radioactivity The process by which the nuclei of certain atoms lose energy by emitting radiation.

second-wave feminism A period of activism starting in the United States in the 1960s where women demanded more than voting rights, including reproductive and workplace rights regardless of their sexual orientation or race.

shaman Someone who communicates with higher powers or spirits.

subordinate A person who occupies a lower position than someone else.

transmutation The act of changing the state or form of one thing into another.

vocation A strong feeling toward one's chosen career path; a calling or a mission.

FURTHER READING

BOOKS

Diehn, Andi, and Lena Chadhok. *Technology: Cool Women Who Code*. White River Junction, VT: Nomad Press, 2015.

Faulkner, Nicholas. *101 Women of STEM*. New York, NY: Britannica Educational Publishing/Rosen Educational Services, 2017.

Hagler, Gina. *Ada Lovelace*. New York, NY: Rosen Publishing, 2015.

Indovino, Shaina Carmel. *Women in Information Technology*. Broomall, PA: Mason Crest, 2014.

Indovino, Shaina Carmel. *Women Inventors*. Broomall, PA: Mason Crest, 2014.

Schatz, Kate, and Miriam Klein Stahl. *Rad American Women A-Z: Rebels, Trailblazers, and Visionaries Who Shaped Our History...and Our Future!* San Francisco, CA: City Lights Publishing, 2015.

Staley, Erin. *Grace Murray Hopper*. New York, NY: Rosen Publishing, 2016.

Swaby, Rachel. *Headstrong: 52 Women Who Changed Science—and the World*. New York, NY: Broadway Books, 2015.

WEBSITES

Famous Women Inventors
www.women-inventors.com
Read more about modern women inventors such as Mary Anderson, Dr. Temple Grandin, and Hedy Lamarr.

Global Women Inventors and Innovators Network
www.gwiin.com
This nonprofit organization provides support and information to help women succeed in the global marketplace.

Women in Technology International
www.witi.com
WITI is the world's leading trade association for women in technology and provides networking opportunities and resources.

INDEX